TEN RUSSIAN POETS

Ten Russian Poets

SURVIVING THE TWENTIETH CENTURY

EDITED BY
Richard McKane

*With translations by Richard McKane
and Vladimir Baskayev, Kitty Hunter Blair,
Belinda Cooke and Michael Molnar*

ANVIL PRESS POETRY
IN ASSOCIATION WITH SURVIVORS' POETRY

Published in 2003
by Anvil Press Poetry Ltd
Neptune House 70 Royal Hill London SE10 8RF
www.anvilpresspoetry.com
in association with Survivors' Poetry
Diorama Arts Centre 34 Osnaburgh Street London NW1 3ND

Selection and editorial matter copyright © Richard McKane 2003
Translations and notes copyright © 2003 Vladimir Baskayev, Michael Basker,
Kitty Hunter Blair, Belinda Cooke, Richard McKane and Michael Molnar

This book is published with financial assistance
from The Arts Council of England

Designed and set in Monotype Ehrhardt by Anvil
Printed aand bound in England
by Cromwell Press, Trowbridge, Wiltshire

ISBN 0 85646 328 0

A catalogue record for this book
is available from the British Library

Contents

VELIMIR KHLEBNIKOV
Translated anonymously
Introduced by Richard McKane
THE 1910S

OSIP MANDELSTAM
Translated by Richard McKane
Introduced by Michael Basker
THE 1920S

BORIS POPLAVSKY
Translated by Belinda Cooke and by Richard McKane
Introduced by Belinda Cooke
THE 1930S

DANIEL ANDREYEV
Introduced by Richard McKane
THE 1940S

Translated by Richard McKane and Vladimir Baskayev

Translated by Richard McKane and Belinda Cooke

From RISING OF THE SOUL

ARSENY TARKOVSKY
Translated by Kitty Hunter Blair and by Richard McKane
Introduced by Kitty Hunter Blair
THE 1950S

LEONID ARONZON
Translated and introduced by Richard McKane
THE 1960S

ANONYMOUS POET FROM
THE ARSENAL MENTAL PRISON HOSPITAL
Translated and introduced by Richard McKane
THE 1970S

Note

Where a poet's section contains translations by more than one person, the translators are identified in the text by their initials in square brackets. In the case of Daniel Andreyev, only the version not by the main translators is identified.

Introduction

THIS BOOK BRINGS together ten Russian poets under one cover. Each poet is represented by poems from one decade of the twentieth century. Apart from Osip Mandelstam (the twenties) and perhaps Velimir Khlebnikov (the tens) the poets may be entirely new in translation to the majority of readers. In many cases the very survival of their poems has only occurred in Russian in the last years. *Glasnost* opened up Kuzmin, Poplavsky, Andreyev, Aronzon, Krivulin – and by the time Katia Kapovich was writing her poems in the 1990s, the whole picture of publishing and readership had changed radically. I had a personal involvement in the publication of Aronzon in Russian and English, and the Arsenal poems in English. During Aronzon's lifetime he did not publish a single poem. The selection may seem to reflect my own enthusiasms in reading Russian poetry, but in effect this is an alternative canon, neither in the Soviet mould nor in that of the Russian poetry already known in the West. My colleagues helped unstintingly. A translator who wishes to remain anonymous supplied translations of Khlebnikov, arguably one of the most difficult poets of the twentieth century: and as is only right, hands on to the reader some of the problems (archaisms are not the only ones) which even translation and commentary cannot solve. I respect this translator's dedication to Khlebnikov.

Michael Basker, who wrote the introduction and commentary for my translations of Nikolay Gumilyov (*The Pillar of Fire*, 1999), was in his element introducing Osip Mandelstam and writing the notes. With his scholarly commentary on the complete poems of 1921–1925, the most detailed in any language, I wanted to add something for readers of Mandelstam, who have formerly found this cycle of poems only partially translated in the selections available. It is a vital part of an unpublished Collected Poems of Osip Mandelstam, which I have translated – the later poems with Elizabeth McKane, who also helped me with several Mandelstam translations in this book – for which Michael Basker is preparing a commentary. I also remembered my Oxford friend Jennifer Baines saying that Nadezhda Mandelstam frequently said that this was her favourite period of Osip Mandelstam's poetry.

I came to Kuzmin late, in the mid-1990s, and with the 'Alexandrian Songs' drew parallels with my reading of Cavafy in the 1960s. The 'Library of the Poet' text I used was published in 1990 in a print run of 4,000, minuscule compared with the four poets Anna Akhmatova, Boris Pasternak, Osip Mandelstam and Marina Tsvetayeva, who were published in full in the late 1980s in editions of millions, and the specifically 'Soviet' poets, none of whom, I think it is fair to claim, are represented in this collection though the Soviet Union ran for over seventy years of the last century.

Kuzmin stands outside the main movements of the twentieth century, though he started out rather late in life, when Symbolism was flourishing, but he could be said to have influenced the OBERIU, an acronym that sounds ungainly in English for the grouping of poets including Zabolotsky (now brilliantly translated by Daniel Weissbort in *Selected Poems*, Carcanet, 1999), Kharms, Vvedensky and Vaginov, whom he rated highly. It is possible to see affinities in Aronzon with the OBERIU, though he wrote forty years later. Of the other movements of the 1910s, Khlebnikov is a futurist (and has always interested me more than Vladimir Mayakovsky) and Mandelstam is an Acmeist.

Boris Poplavsky, poet of Parisian cafés and melancholia, hiding behind his dark glasses, has been discovered for the English reader in this selection by Belinda Cooke, with some extra translations by myself. I had heard of him through Arkady Rovner and Victoria Andreyeva, the publishers of *Gnosis* magazine (New York and Moscow) and my collected Aronzon. Belinda Cooke shared photocopies of the Berkeley Poplavsky with me, then Michael Molnar lent me two volumes of Poplavsky and I lent him my two volumes of Krivulin. I say this to establish the closeness between the translators and the difficulties (still) of obtaining some Russian texts, though I have found the bookshop Thorntons of Oxford most supportive for one who doesn't travel regularly to Russia.

Daniel Andreyev has revolved in my mind since the late seventies. I instinctively knew he was a fine poet from extracts of *The Rose of the World*, but it was only in the 1990s that a good edition of his poems was published and that I met Vladimir Baskayev, an artist and film-script writer, who shared my passion for his writing and philosophy. Co-translation of especially difficult poets can mean that 1+1 equals more than 2. In Andreyev's case the poems survived by a miracle and the dedication of his wife. None of the poets are bound by time, but the poetry within their decade personifies it, yet sometimes reacting against it.

Perhaps the most lasting breakthrough from *glasnost* and the collapse of the Soviet Union has been and will be no more and no less than the discovery and rediscovery of Russian literature, once banned or ignored. Editions may be small but the publications in Russia are there: these are exciting times, the process is irreversible. Even Poplavsky, who wrote his poems in exile in Paris, has come home to roost in Russia, and a poet like Katia Kapovich, who lives and teaches in the USA can travel to teach in St Petersburg and publish in Russian, both in America and Russia.

I feel a particular empathy for Arseny Tarkovsky. For decades he was known only as a translator. Akhmatova admired his poetry – his first book was destroyed after the Zhdanov decree of 1946, which singled out his friend Akhmatova and Zoshchenko for attack. Kitty Hunter Blair, who translated Arseny's son Andrei the filmmaker's *Sculpting in Time* (Faber), has provided her translations of Arseny Tarkovsky's timeless poems from the crucial decade of the fifties, and I have added my own. We are both privileged to know Arseny's daughter Marina, whose book *Fragments of a Mirror* has come out in Russia, and we recently read with her at the Pushkin Club (of which I am co-chair) in London with Tarkovsky's friend Peter Norman, who has also translated him. In fact bilingual poetry readings at the Pushkin Club have been a tremendous stimulus to the translation of these poets.

Every translator has his or her favourite poet and when I first came across some of Aronzon's poems in 1975 I realized very clearly that Aronzon was speaking to me in a voice that I could make my own. I became his translator and, since he died young, his first interpreter and advocate.

The anonymous poet from the Arsenal Mental Prison Hospital in Leningrad is not a figment of anyone's imagination, but an example of the poetry of survival and the survival of poetry in the tradition of Irina Ratushinskaya and Nizametdin Akhmetov, who both wrote poems in prison or camp. He can have no biography and probably was not a dissident: he is the unknown poet of the mental hospital, peculiarly Russian, yet soul-wrenchingly universal.

Viktor Krivulin was a friend of Michael Molnar's and mine. He introduced both Mandelstam's *Moscow Notebooks* and *The Voronezh Notebooks* (Bloodaxe Books) which I translated with Elizabeth McKane. A prolific poet, and late in life essayist and publicist, his first books in Russia were only published after *glasnost*. I remember a gathering of poets at his flat in Leningrad in 1990 – I had not visited the city since I was a schoolboy in 1963. We took it in turn to read poems into little hand-held cassette recorders. Viktor had translated three or four of my poems into Russian: the boot was on the other foot! Viktor talked about his enchantments and disenchantments with poetry and his trips to the West, the differences and similarities in our 'poetry systems'. He had been at the centre of underground poetry in Leningrad since the 1960s – times had changed. My friend Yefim Slavinsky, who made a conscious decision not to become a poet in Leningrad in the 1960s, said to me at the end of the millennium: 'I now realize the '60s have finally ended.'

Katia Kapovich, who draws the book to a close, gives evidence that Russian poetry is still flourishing, still complicated, lyrical and demanding – still Russian, though an increasing number of poets are writing abroad. On a more sombre note, these ten poets survived the twentieth century in different senses, but one should also bear in mind the casualties: not just the poets who died young like Gumilyov, Khlebnikov, Poplavsky and Aronzon, but the poets who were silenced before they even wrote, and those, in a country that still loves poetry deeply though under attack by consumerism, who will now never follow the paths that were trod by the feet of these poets throughout the twentieth century. The stars of differing magnitudes shine through the surrounding darkness. I sincerely believe that a reading of these ten Russian poets teaches more about Russia, even more about that almost forgotten cliché, the Russian soul, than do the figures of Lenin, Stalin, Khrushchev, Brezhnev, Gorbachev and Yeltsin rolled into one. But then I am biased.

As Akhmatova wrote just after the end of World War II on the brink of the Cold War: 'Away with time, away with space'. She knew in her lifetime of the acceleration of 'The Flight of Time'. Of all the written arts poetry is the most flexible, because it is usually ahead of its time. Translation is change or exchange and it may take decades of work by translators to fill in the missing panels of the tapestry of Russian poetry of the twentieth century.

I would like to thank, on behalf of all the translators, the Arts Council of England for a grant under the Arts for Everyone scheme and Survivors' Poetry for making that and this book a reality. I dedicate my translations in this book to the memory of my friend, the poet Victoria Andreyeva.

RICHARD MCKANE
London, May 2000–March 2003

Mikhail Kuzmin
(6 October 1872–1 March 1936)

Translated by Richard McKane

THE 'ALEXANDRIAN SONGS' that form a section of Kuzmin's first book *Nets* were written in the mid-1900s, ten years after Kuzmin's travels to Egypt and Alexandria. About that time Constantine Cavafy was beginning his more hermetic writing career in that very same city. The Russian poet Georgy promised me his article on Kuzmin's 'Alexandrian Songs' and Cavafy but I have not received it. The connection is not made in John Malmstad and Nikolay Bogomolov's excellent biography: *Mikhail Kuzmin: A Life in Art* (Harvard University Press, 1999), but would be based not only on both poets being gay, but also their treatment of antiquity, especially Hellenism. It is very unlikely that they were conscious of each others' existence or writing.

Kuzmin travelled to Egypt in 1895, after an attempted suicide, with a friend 'Prince Georges' who was to die young in Vienna, shortly after the Egypt trip, of heart disease. Rather than calling Kuzmin 'the Russian Cavafy', or 'the northern Oscar Wilde' (Kuzmin is on record of having attacked Wilde in conversation), his poems, plays, diaries and prose lift him into the Pantheon of Russian twentieth-century writers: 'His modern editor, Vladimir Markov, is not alone in equating his best prose with the finest of the twentieth century. The same can confidently be claimed for his magnificent later verse', Michael Basker writes and later in his article on Kuzmin in *A Reference Guide to Russian Literature* he says Kuzmin had an 'ideological independence from Symbolism, Acmeism and Futurist primitivism, despite close personal and creative ties with leading representatives of each.'

Why is Kuzmin's work virtually not translated in this country? Ardis in the USA brought out two books of prose and poetry (1972 and 1980) translated by Neil Granoien and Michael Green, and Michael Green respectively; and Robert Stanilov in New York is working on a translation of *The Trout Breaks the Ice* (1929). Olga

Sedakova, the fine contemporary Russian poet (her book *The Wild Rose* is published bilingually in my translation by Approach Books, London), when asked who her favourite Russian poet was, answered 'Kuzmin'. It was this stimulus alone that started me reading Kuzmin in the 1990s – and translating him.

Born in 1872 in Yaroslavl on the Volga, Kuzmin was to have a parallel career to his literary one in music, which he concentrated on from childhood. The 'Alexandrian Songs', mainly written in free verse, had a piano accompaniment. The whole cycle, Kuzmin's preferred form, is translated here. After further travel in Italy, and a period of retreat to Old Believer settlements round the Volga and in northern Russia, Kuzmin became actively involved from the early 1900s in the literary, musical and artistic life of St Petersburg. He wrote the preface to Anna Akhmatova's first book *Evening* (1912) but later she was to turn against him, including demonizing him in 'Poem Without a Hero'. Her criticisms of him are discussed in the Malmstad and Bogomolov biography (pp. 221–5). He had had an affair with Vsevolod Knyazev, the bisexual poet and 'cornet of dragoons' of 'Poem Without a Hero', who later committed suicide. From 1913 he was to have a relationship up to his death in 1936 with Yury Yurkun. His books suffered a similar fate to those of his former friend Nikolay Gumilyov, being unpublished in the Soviet Union from 1929 to the 1980s.

Kuzmin's poems, always sensitive and without reproaches, are radiant with a 'beautiful clarity'. The main collection in the Novaya Biblioteka Poeta (edited by Nikolay Bogomolov) runs to 600 pages. Given that good Russian texts are now available it is high time that translators should begin to pay attention to him. At the end of their Introduction Malmstad and Bogomolov tell the reality that Kuzmin was 'celebrated, abandoned, and rediscovered because great.'

The translator would like to thank Michael Basker and Robert Stanilov for their useful suggestions on these translations.

Richard McKane

Alexandrian Songs

To N.P. Feofilaktov

I Introduction

1

Like a mother's song
over a baby's cradle,
like an echo in the mountains
of a shepherd's horn in the morning,
like the distant surf
of a familiar sea, not seen for ages:
this is how your name sounds to me
thrice blissful
            Alexandria!

Like a broken whisper
of love's confessions under the oaks,
like a mysterious rustling
of sacred, shady groves,
like the tambourine of great Cybele,
like the distant thunder and the cooing of doves
your name sounds to me
thrice wise
            Alexandria!

Like the sound of the trumpet before battle,
the screeches of eagles over the abyss,
the noise of the wings of flying Nike
your name sounds to me
thrice great:
            Alexandria!

2

When they say to me 'Alexandria'
I see the white walls of a house,
a small garden with a bed of gilly-flower,
the pale sun of an autumn evening
and I hear the playing of distant flutes.

When they say to me 'Alexandria'
I see the stars over the quietening down city,
drunk sailors in the dark boroughs,
a danseuse dancing 'the wasp',
and I hear the bang of a tambourine and a shouted argument.

When they say to me: 'Alexandria'
I see a pale brown-red sunset over the green sea,
furry twinkling stars
and bright grey eyes under thick eyebrows,
which I also see even then
when they don't say to me: 'Alexandria!'

3

The evening twilight over the warm sea,
lights of the lighthouses in the darkened sky,
the scent of verbena at the end of a feast,
the fresh morning after long vigils,
a walk in the alleys of the spring garden,
screams and laughter of women bathing,
sacred peacocks by the temple of Juno,
sellers of violets, pomegranates and lemons,
the doves coo, the sun shines,
when I see you, my native city!

II *Love*

1

When I first met you
my poor memory does not remember:
was it morning or daytime,
evening or late at night?
I only remember your paleish cheeks,
grey eyes under dark eyebrows
and a blue collar at your tanned neck,
and it seems to me that I saw this in early childhood,
although I am much older than you.

2

You are like a youth who accompanies a soothsayer:
you read everything in my heart,
you can tell all that I think,
you know all my thoughts,
but your knowledge is not great here
and not many words are needed here,
no need for a mirror, nor brazier:
in my heart, thinking and thoughts,
all in one sound with different voices:
'I love you, I love you forever!'

3

I must have been conceived at noon,
I must have been born at noon,
and I've loved the shining rays
of the sun from my early years.
Since I saw your eyes
I've become cold to the sun:
why should I love just that one
when there are two in your eyes?

4

People see the gardens with houses
and the sea, blood-red from the sunset,
people see seagulls over the sea
and women on flat roofs,
people see warriors in armour
and pie sellers in the square,
people see the sun and the stars,
the streams and the bright little rivers,
but I see everywhere only
paleish tanned cheeks,
grey eyes under dark eyebrows,
and an incomparably graceful waist –
so eyes of lovers see
that which the wise heart orders they should see.

5

When I go out of the house in the morning
I think, looking at the sun:
'How like you it is
when you bathe in the stream
or look at the distant back-gardens!'
And when I look in the hot noontime
at that same burning sun,
I think about you, my joy.
'How it is like you
when you ride through the crowded street!'
And when I look at the tender sunsets
you come into my memory,
when pale from caresses, you fall asleep
and close your darkened eyelids.

6

Not in vain did we read the theologians,
not for nothing did we study the orators,
we know the meaning of every word
and we can interpret them in seven ways.
I can find the four virtues in your body
and the seven sins, of course;
and I will willingly accept the beatitudes;
but of all the words two do not change:
when I look into your grey eyes
and say: 'I love' – every orator
understands only 'I love' – and nothing more.

7

If I was an ancient warlord
and subjugated Ethiopia and the Persians
and overthrew the Pharaohs,
I would build myself a pyramid
higher than Kheops
and would be
more famous than everyone in Egypt.

If I was a cunning thief
and raided the temple of Mekanu
and sold gems to Alexandrian Jews,
I would buy lands and mills
and would be
richer than everyone living in Egypt.

If I was a second Antinous
who drowned in the sacred Nile
I would drive everyone mad with my beauty,
temples would be built for me in my lifetime,
and I would be
more powerful than everyone living in Egypt.

If I was a great wise man
I would spend all my money,
refuse positions and jobs,
I would guard others' gardens
and I would be
freer than everyone living in Egypt.

If I was your last slave
imprisoned in a cellar
and saw once or twice a year
the gold pattern of your sandals,
when by chance you passed the dungeons,
I would be
more happy than everyone living in Egypt.

III *She*

1

We were four sisters, four sisters were we,
we all four loved but we all had different 'becauses':
one loved because her father and mother ordered her to,
the second loved because her lover was rich,
the third loved because he was a famous painter,
but I loved because I loved.

We were four sisters, four sisters were we,
we all desired but our desires were different:
one desired to bring up children and cook porridge,
the second desired to put on new dresses every day,
the third desired that everyone talk about her,
but I desired to love and be loved.

We were four sisters, four sisters were we,
we all fell out of love but we all had different reasons,
one fell out of love because her husband died,
the second fell out of love because her friend went bankrupt,
the third fell out of love because the artist dumped her,
and I fell out of love because I fell out of love.

We were four sisters, four sisters were we,
but perhaps we were not four, but five?

2

In spring the poplar changes its leaves,
Adonis returns in spring
from the kingdom of the dead ...
My joy where do you go in spring?

In spring everybody goes boating on the sea,
or riding in the gardens round about
on swift horses ...
but who can I row with in a light boat?

In spring everyone dresses up in bright dresses
and walks in couples in the meadows with flowers
to gather violets . . .
but as for me, do you order me to sit at home?

3

It's a holiday today:
all the bushes are in bloom,
the blackcurrants are in time
and the lotus floats in the pond like a hive.
If you want
let's chase each other
down the path, planted round with yellow roses,
to the lake where the goldfish swim.
If you want
let's go to the summerhouse,
they'll give us sweet drinks,
pies and hazelnuts,
a boy will wave a fan
and we will look
at the distant back-gardens with their sweetcorn.
If you want
I'll sing a Greek song to the playing of the harp,
on condition:
'No dozing off, and don't forget
to praise the singer and the musician at the end of the song.'
If you want
I'll dance 'the wasp'
alone on the green lawn,
for you alone.
If you want
I'll treat you to currants, not handling them,
and you'll take them with lips from lips,
red berries,
and kisses
altogether.

If you want, if you want
we will count the stars,
and the one who gets it wrong – will be punished.
It's a holiday today,
the whole garden is in bloom,
come, my love, my eyes feast on you,
and make this holiday a feast day.

4

Is it a lie
that pearls dissolve in vinegar,
that verbena freshens the air,
that the cooing of doves is tender?

Is it a lie
that I am the first lady in Alexandria
when it comes to the luxury of expensive outfits,
when it comes to valuable white horses and silver harness,
along the length of black, cunningly-woven plaits?
that no one knows more craftily how to make-up eyes
and to endow every finger
with a separate aroma?

Is it a lie
that from the time I saw you,
I can see nothing more,
hear nothing more,
desire nothing more
than to see your eyes,
grey under your thick eyebrows,
than to hear your voice?

Is it a lie
that I myself gave you a quince that I'd bitten,
that I sent you experienced confidantes,
that I paid your debts before
I sold the estate
and exchanged all my outfits

for love potions?
And is it a lie
that all this was in vain?

But let it be true
that pearls dissolve in vinegar,
that verbena freshens the air,
that the cooing of doves is tender,
it will be true,
it will be true,
that too,
that you will love me!

5

Imitation of P. Louÿs

There were four that month
but there was only one that I loved.

The first completely ruined himself over me,
every hour he sent me new gifts
and sold his last mill to buy me bracelets
which clinked when I danced – he stabbed himself,
but he was not the one that I loved.

The second wrote thirty elegies in my honour
that were famous as far as Rome, where it was said
that my cheeks were like the morning dawns
and my tresses were like the canopy of night,
but he was not the one that I loved.

The third, ah, the third was so handsome
that his own sister choked herself with her hair
out of fear of falling in love with him;
he stood day and night at my doorstep
pleading for me to say: 'Come in'. but I kept silent,
because he was not the one that I loved.

You were not rich, did not talk about dawns and nights,
were not handsome,
and when I threw you a carnation on the feast day of Adonis
you looked dispassionately with your bright eyes,
but you were the one that I loved.

6

I don't know how it happened:
my mother had gone out to the bazaar;
I swept clean the house
and sat at the loom to weave.
I didn't (I swear), I didn't sit at the threshold,
but at the high window.
I wove and sang;
what else? Nothing.
I don't know how it happened:
my mother had gone out to the bazaar.
I don't know how it happened:
it was a high window.
He must have rolled up a rock,
or climbed on a tree,
or stood on a bench.
He said:
'I thought it was a robin redbreast,
but this is Penelope.
Why are you at home? Hello!'
'Why are you clambering about in the eaves like a bird
and not writing your sweet scrolls in court?'
'Yesterday we went by boat on the Nile –
my head aches.'
'It obviously does not ache enough
to dissuade you from night revels.'
I don't know how it happened:
it was a high window.

I don't know how it happened:
I thought he couldn't reach it.

'Do you see what I've got in my mouth?'
'What would you have in your mouth
other than strong teeth and a prattling tongue,
and follies in your head.'
'Look, I've got a rose in my mouth.'
'What do you mean, a rose?'
'I'll give it to you, if you wish,
only you must get it yourself.'
I got up on my tiptoes,
I got up on a bench,
I got up on the firm loom base,
I got the crimson rose
and he, unfittingly, said:
'With your mouth, your mouth,
only from my mouth to yours,
no, not with your hands, your hands!'
Perhaps my lips
touched his, I don't know.
I don't know how it happened,
I thought he couldn't reach.
I don't know how it happened
I was weaving and singing.
I wasn't (I swear), I wasn't sitting by the threshold,
it was a high window:
who could reach there?
When my mother returned, she said:
'What's this Zoya,
you've weaved a rose instead of a narcissus?
What's going on in your head?'
I don't know how it happened.

IV *Wisdom*

1

I asked the wise ones of the universe:
'Why does the sun heat?
Why does the wind blow?
Why are people born?'

The wise ones of the universe answered:
'The sun heats
so the wheat will grow for food
and so the people will die from the plague.
The wind blows
so it can guide boats to a distant harbour
and so it can bury caravans with sand.
People are born
so they will part from sweet life
and so from them others can be born for death.

'Why did the gods create everything like that?'
For the same reason
that they gave you the desire
to ask vain questions.

2

What can I do
when the blood-red of the evening clouds
is in the greenish sky,
when the moon is visible on the left
and a huge furry star,
the harbinger of the night,
swiftly pales,
dissolves
right before one's eyes?
When the path down the broad road
between the trees, past the mills
which were once mine

but have been exchanged into your bracelets,
where we are riding with you,
ends beyond the turn-off,
even as a welcoming
house
at this very moment.
That my poems
dear to me
as to Callimachus
and every other great one,
where I lay down love and all tenderness
and thoughts made light from the gods,
the joy of my mornings
when the sky is clear
and the jasmine smells at the window,
tomorrow
will they be forgotten as everything?
That I will stop seeing
your face,
hear your voice?
That wine will be drunk down,
that fragrances will evaporate
and the most precious fabrics
will fade away
in centuries to come?
Am I really going to love less
these dear, fragile things
for their decaying?

    3

How I love, eternal gods,
this beautiful world!
How I love the sun, the reeds
and the sparkle of the greenish sea
through the slender acacia branches!
How I love books (my friends),
the silence of the lonely house

and the view from the window
to the distant melon gardens!
How I love the motleyness of the crowd on the square,
shouts, singing and the sun,
the happy laughter of boys playing with a ball!
The return home
after happy strolls
late in the evening
under the first stars,
past the brightly-lit hotels
with a friend, already distant!
How I love, eternal gods,
bright sadness,
love till tomorrow,
death without pity for life,
where everything is sweet,
the life I love, I swear by Dionysus,
with all the power of my heart
and dear flesh!

4

It is sweet to die
on the field of battle
to the whistle of arrows and spears,
when the trumpet calls,
and the sun shines
at midday,
dying for the glory of the fatherland
and hearing around
'Farewell, hero!'
It is sweet to die
as a venerable old man
in the same house,
in the same bed
where grandfathers were born and died
surrounded by children
who've already become husbands,

and to hear around:
'Farewell, father!'
But it's still sweeter,
still wiser,
having spent all one's estate,
having sold your last mill,
for her,
whom tomorrow you could have forgotten,
and having returned
after a happy stroll
to the house you have already sold,
to have supper
and having read a story of Apuleius
for the hundred and first time,
in a warm fragrant bath,
not hearing any farewells,
to slice open your veins;
that at the ceiling by the long window
there should be a smell of gilly-flower,
the sunset should shine
and the flutes be heard in the distance.

5

Sun, sun,
divine Ra-Helios,
the hearts of kings and heroes
are joyful from you,
sacred horses neigh to you,
hymns are sung to you in Heliopolis;
when you shine
the lizards crawl onto the rocks
and the boys go laughing
to bathe in the Nile.
Sun, sun,
I am the pale scribe,
the library hermit,
but I love you, sun, no less

than the tanned sailor,
smelling of fish and salt water,
and no less
than his inured heart triumphs
at your regal rising
from the ocean,
my heart trembles
when your dusty, flaming ray
slips
through the narrow window by the ceiling
onto the written page
and my slender, yellowish hand,
highlighting with vermilion
the first letter of a hymn to you,
O Ra–Helios, sun!

V *Fragments*

I

My son,
the time for parting has come.
You won't see me for a long time,
you won't hear me for a long time,
and was it not long ago
that your grandfather brought you from the desert
and you said as you looked at me:
'Is this the god Fta, grandpa?'
Now you yourself are like the god Fta
and you are going into the wide world
and you are going without me,
but Isis is with you everywhere.
Do you remember the walks
down the alleys of acacia
in the courtyard of the temple
when you talked to me about your love
and cried and your tanned face turned pale?
Do you remember how we watched
the stars from the temple walls
and the town quietened down,
close but far?
I'm not talking about divine secrets.
Tomorrow other students will come to me
and they won't say: 'Is this the god Fta?' –
because I'm older now
whereas you have become like the god Fta,
but I won't forget you
and my thoughts,
my prayers
will accompany you into the wide world,
O my son.

2

When they led me through the garden
then through a series of rooms on the right and left
to a square chamber
where under a violet light through the curtains
there lay
in precious clothes
with bracelets and rings
a woman, beautiful as Gator,
with made-up eyes and black tresses:
I stopped.
She said to me:
'Well?'
and I didn't speak
and smiling she looked at me
and threw me a yellow flower
from her hair.
I picked it up and lifted it to my lips
and she looked askance and said:
'Is this why you came,
boy,
to kiss a flower thrown onto the floor?'
'Yes, queen,' I uttered
and the whole chamber burst
into the ringing laughter of the woman
and her serving women:
together they clapped their hands,
together they laughed
like the sistra at the feast of Isis,
struck all at once by the priests.

3

What rain!
Our sail is drenched,
you can't even tell that it's striped.
The rouge streaked down your cheeks

and you were like a dyer from Tyre.
Fearfully we crossed
the threshold of the low mud-brick hut of the coal-heaver,
the owner with a scar on his forehead
shoved away the dirty scabby kids
with their sick eyes
and putting his stump hand before you
shook the dust off his apron
with a slap and said:
'Will sir eat a pancake?'
An old black woman
rocked a baby and sang:
'If I was a pharaoh
I would buy myself two pears:
one I'd give to my friend,
the other I'd eat myself.'

4

Once more I saw the city where I was born
and spent my distant youth;
I knew
that none of my relatives and friends were left there,
I knew
that there was no memory of me left there,
but the houses, the twists of the streets,
the distant, green sea –
they all reminded me
of what does not change:
the distant days of childhood,
youth's dreams and plans,
love that flew away like smoke.
A stranger to everyone,
without money,
not knowing where to rest my head,
I found myself in a distant quarter of the city
where lights shone through the lowered shutters
and I could hear singing and tambourines

from the inner rooms.
By a lowered curtain
a beautiful, curly-haired boy was standing
and when I slowed my walk since I was tired
he said to me:
'Abba,
it looks like you don't know where you're going
and that you have no friends.
Come in here:
there's everything here
for strangers to forget loneliness
and you can find
a happy, carefree girlfriend
with a supple body and fragrant hair.'
I slowed up, thinking about something else
and he continued, smiling:
'If that doesn't attract you,
wanderer,
there are other delights here
which a bold and wise heart shouldn't miss.'
As I crossed the threshold I cast off my sandals
lest I should bring into the house of delight
the sacred sand of the desert.
Glancing at that door-keeper
I saw
that he was almost naked
and we went further down the corridor
where from far away
the sound of tambourines came to meet us.

5

Three times I saw him face to face.
The first time I was walking in the garden,
sent to fetch lunch for my fellow soldiers,
and to take a short cut
I chose the way past the windows of the palace wing:
suddenly I heard the sound of strings

and, as I am a tall man,
in the broad window I easily saw
him:
he was sitting sad and alone,
running his slender fingers over the lyre strings
and a white dog
was lying by his feet without snarling,
and only the splash of the fountain
mixed with the music.
When he sensed me looking at him
he put down the lyre
and lifted his lowered face.
His beauty and his silence
in the empty chamber at midday
cast a magic spell!
I crossed myself and ran in terror
away from the window ...
Then I was on guard duty in Lekhie
and standing in the passage
leading to the room of the king's astrologer.
The moon cast a bright square on the floor
and the bronze buckles on my shoes
sparkled
as I passed the bright light.
I stopped
as I heard footsteps.
Three men came out
from the inner chamber
with a slave leading with a torch
and he was among them.
He was pale
but it seemed to me
that the room lit up
not from the torch but his face.
As he passed he looked at me
and said: 'I've seen you somewhere, friend.'
And he went away into the astrologer's rooms.
His white clothes had long gone

and the torch light had vanished
but I just stood there not moving nor breathing.
When I lay in barracks
I felt
Marcius, who slept beside me,
touch my hand with the usual touch,
I pretended to be asleep.
Then one evening
we met again.
We were bathing
not far from Caesar's field tents
when we heard screaming.
We ran there but saw it was too late.
The body dragged from the water
lay on the sand
and the same unearthly face,
that face of a magician,
looked out with unclosed eyes.
The Emperor hastened from afar,
devastated by the terrible news,
and I stood there and saw nothing,
not sensing the tears, forgotten since childhood,
flowing down my cheeks.
All night I whispered prayers,
saw visions of my homeland Asia and Nikodemia,
and the voices of angels sang:
'Hosannah!
A new god
is given to humans!'

VI *Kanop Songs*

1

Life is free and easy in Kanop:
let's go there, my friend.
We'll sit in a light rowboat
and get there without difficulty.
The hotels still stand
by the calm bank –
luring the travellers to them
with their cool terraces.
Let's get a room
together my friend;
we'll deck ourselves in wreaths
and sit holding hands.
We don't need lessons, my friend,
in how to kiss sweetly:
sacred, gracious Kanop
can cure all sorrows.

2

Am I not like an apple tree,
a blossoming apple tree,
tell me, my girls?
Isn't my hair as curly
as its topmost branches?
Isn't my figure as harmonious
as its trunk?
My arms are supple as branches.
My legs are strong as roots.
Are my kisses not sweeter than the sweet apple?
But oh!
But oh!
the young men stand in the round dance,
eating the fruit off that apple tree,
my fruit,

my fruit
only one can eat at a time.

3

Ah, our garden, our vineyard
should be watered more often
and the dry twigs of the apple tree
should be pruned more often.
In our modest little garden
there are flowers and grapes;
whoever sees the clusters of bunches
will be happy at heart.
The wicket-gate between the bushes
beckons to the passer-by –
hospitable Zeus
orders it to remain open.
We will let everyone through the gate,
we will open the garden to everyone,
we're not niggardly: everyone can
take our ripe grapes.

4

Aphrodite is searching for Adonis,
roaming by the seashore
like a lioness.
The goddess Aphrodite became weary –
she lay down to sleep by the sea –
but could not sleep –
she dreams of white Adonis,
his clear gaze is deadened,
lack-lustre.
Aphrodite jumped up, hardly breathing
and she doesn't feel her tiredness:
it's gone.
She ran straight to the place
where the body of Adonis lay

by the sea.
Aphrodite screamed loud screams
and the waves murmured noisily
echoing her.

5

Circle, circle:
hold
hands firmer!
Sounds
of the ringing sistrum carry, carry
and resound languorously in the groves.
Does the Nile fisherman know
when he throws
his net in the sea what he will catch?
Does the hunter know
what he'll come across,
will he kill the prey that he aims at?
Does the landowner know
whether the hail will lay low
his wheat and his young vineyard?
What do we know?
What is known to us?
What are we sad about?
Circle, circle:
hold hands firmer!
Sounds
of the ringing sistrum will carry, carry,
resound languorously in the groves.
We know
that all is false, all goes away from us irrevocably.
We know
that all is decay
and only inconstancy is unchanging.
We know
that the sweet body
is given only to decay later.
This is what we know,

this is what we love,
let's give a triple kiss
since it's all so fragile.
Circle, circle:
hold
hands firmer.
Sounds
of the ringing sistrum will carry, carry,
resound languorously in the groves.

VII *Conclusion*

Ah, I am leaving Alexandria
and will not see her for a long time!
I will see Cyprus, dear to the Goddess's heart.
I'll see Tyre, Ephesus and Smyrna,
I'll see Athens – my youth's dream,
Corinth and distant Byzantium
and the crown of all my desires,
the aim of all my yearnings –
I'll see great Rome!
I'll see all of them, but not you!
Ah, I am leaving you, my joy,
and I won't see you for a very long time!
I'll see a variety of beauties,
I'll look my fill into many different eyes,
I'll kiss many lips,
I'll caress many locks of hair
and whisper many different names
waiting for rendezvous in many different groves.
I will see them all, but not you!

1905–1908

Velimir Khlebnikov

(28 October 1885–28 June 1922)

Translated anonymously, edited by Richard McKane

VIKTOR VLADIMIROVICH KHLEBNIKOV – he later changed his name to Velimir Khlebnikov – was born in a village in the Astrakhan Province on the eastern border of Russia in the Kalmyk steppe. His father was a natural scientist and ornithologist, and indeed Velimir was to publish several papers on ornithology. The family moved to Astrakhan city which is near where the Volga flows into the Caspian. His eastern origins were to be a huge influence on him.

In 1903 he went to Kazan University first to study Physics and Mathematics and then natural sciences. Kazan was the main town in the Tatar area. In 1908 he went to Petersburg to become a writer. He had already read the French Symbolists. In Petersburg he regarded Mikhail Kuzmin as his Master and also went to the Symbolist Vyacheslav Ivanov's famous Tower where the poets of the day gathered.

As the editors of *Tvoreniya*, up till the late nineties the best edition of Khlebnikov, say: 'The history of his life is full of moving from town to town, from one chance haven to another. He had no home, no fixed work and most of the time no money.' He lived a nomadic life with friends in Kharkov and Rostov, Baku and Moscow. The year before his death he went with a Red Army expeditionary force to Iran, where he was nicknamed 'Gul Mullah', the Priest of Flowers. He died aged 37 in the village of Santalovo in Novgorod Province from a disease picked up in Iran.

1911 was the year of the crisis of Symbolism: Mandelstam, Gumilyov and Akhmatova became the centre of the Acmeist group whereas Khlebnikov, Mayakovsky and others became known as Futurists, although Khlebnikov preferred the title *budetlyanin*, sometimes translated as 'futurian', using the Russian word for future. Khlebnikov demanded that poets be 'fishers of the pearls of the Russian language' and he certainly dived deep into the Russian language, creating new words from Slavonic roots. Much has been

written about Khlebnikov as a 'difficult poet' (critics talk about
'decoding his poems' when in fact there is a clarity of thought) and
this was compounded by his friend Mayakovsky saying that he was
a 'poet for producers', that is, a 'poets' poet'. It was with Kruch-
onykh, Mayakovsky and David Burliuk that Khlebnikov in 1912
launched the iconoclastic manifesto 'A Slap in the Face of Public
Taste'. Mandelstam (who wrote two pre-emptive elegies, included
in this collection, to Khlebnikov in 1921, and who had Khleb-
nikov's books with him when he was arrested for the final time at a
sanatorium in Samatihka in 1938) remarked in 1922 that it was
not language that was Khlebnikov's main obsession, but time.
Khlebnikov records that it was not space that mattered to the
soldier in the trench, but time. Much of his mathematical work on
Time was spent in calculation of catastrophic events, extrapolating
from dates in the past. War was one of his constant themes: his
most fertile period spanned the First World War, the Revolution
and the Civil War. His long poem 'War in a Mousetrap' is the most
developed treatment of war. We have arbitrarily extended his
'decade' to include works up to his death in 1922.

Khlebnikov, unlike other poets in this collection, did not really
write lyric poetry. Often his shorter poems were incorporated into
longer poems (the Russian *poemy*). He wrote long poems, dramatic
works in verse, 'superpoems' (his term) and prose, articles and
letters. Despite his dying young and the loss of many manuscripts
(on the one hand contemporaries describe his neglect of his archive,
on the other they describe, given his condition of grinding poverty
and homelessness, a man travelling with all his manuscripts in a
sack), the totality of his *oeuvre* is staggering and equal to any poet
of the twentieth century. Undoubtedly he wrote for the future, and
his treatment of Islamic themes is unlike any other Russian poet.
That future has now arrived. It is time to read Khlebnikov in the
present and that is one thing that translations can achieve. Leonid
Aronzon in a 1968 diary entry pays him this praise: 'Khlebnikov
deprived me of the possibility of talking about many things,
because he expressed himself about things so that one could only
express oneself about these things in the same way.'

Daniel Andreyev in his cycle 'The Poet's Cross' has a poem to
Khlebnikov which, in conclusion, I'd like to quote in full:

Khlebnikov

Like a musician on the wing –
the invisible master of the storm,
he rushes the Olympian peels of thunder
on the shattered keyboard.
Clanging chords, and the starry genius,
spreading wide the wings of visions,
invades, like death itself,
the cracked vessel of the mind.

Sparse is his everyday life: a bunk, table and chair,
but nonetheless he is a knight, a warrior,
for the weapons of future massacres
rush roaring through his heart.
A hallucinator with childish eyes,
he does not live on this earth,
but he discovered the return of time,
he computed the lever of generations.

Tauriz, Baku, Moscow, Tsarytsin
spit out the ragamuffin
into homelessness, the roads,
the railroad, to the Cossack villages
where the savage wind circles in the dance,
where races grew strong in the open spaces:
there the demons rushed at him
from the Asian plateaux,
from the snow shaking the frontier.

Through the whoops of shamans, tambourines and rings,
having muddled everything, his eye catches
the path of pilgrims wandering
to the shrines of the eternal East.
He is called to become, by the will of Ka,
like a Phoenix of the Russian fire,
the Leader of the Earthly Sphere,
and the almighty has a hand in this.

But the world is empty and life frozen
and hunger gnaws, wears down and aches.
O hunger, death, menacing protector
from ugly mugs and the dances of paranoia,
you alone could correct
the crazy scheme with your sensitive hand.
Avoid the tragedies of the future:
smash the cracked vessel.

1940

The translator of the poems that follow wishes to remain anonymous. Whereas books of Khlebnikov's work have appeared in translation in the States (Paul Schmidt, Gary Kern), this is the first and I hope not the last selection to appear in the UK from this translator.

There are two main editions of Khlebnikov's work published in Russia: *Tvoreniya* edited by M.Ya. Polyakova, V.P. Grigoriev and A.E. Parnis (Sovetsky Pisatel', 1986) and the new Russian six-volume edition (Nasledie; only two volumes had appeared by 2002), which with its excellent commentary goes a long way to solving many of the difficulties for readers and translators. The large volume of essays *Mir Velimira Khlebnikova* (The World of Velimir Khlebnikov: Yazyki Russkoy Kul'tury, 2000) gives a superb view of Khlebnikov. For the English reader Raymond Cooke's *Velimir Khlebnikov: A Critical Study* (CUP, 1987) is invaluable.

Richard McKane

The Zoo Garden

Oh, Garden, Garden!

Where the iron rail is like a father, reminding brothers that they are brothers and preventing bloody quarelling.

Where Germans go to drink beer.

And beauties to sell their bodies.

Where the eagles sit resembling the eternity which is signified by this present day, still lacking its evening.

Where a camel whose high hump lacks a rider knows the riddle of Buddhism and has suppressed the shrug of China.

Where a deer is pure fright, flowering on a rocky slab.

Where people wear all their finery.

And the Germans bloom with health.

Where the black gaze of a swan, which altogether is like winter, but whose black and yellow beak is an autumn grove is a little guarded and mistrustful even of itself.

Where a deep blue peacock trails a tail like Siberia seen from the Pavdin Rock (in the Urals) when the blue lace of the clouds has been thrown and fallen over the gold and green of the forest and all is variously shaded because of the unevenness of the terrain.

Where you want to pluck the tail of a lyre bird and strike its string to sing the praises of Russian deeds.

Where we clench our fist as though it held a sword, and whisper an oath to defend the Russian people at the price of life, of death, of everything.

Where the monkeys get annoyed in various ways and display the various ends of their torsos and, except for the sad and submissive ones, are eternally irritated by the presence of man.

Where the elephants posture like mountains that twist during an earthquake and beg food from children ... and squat as though begging alms.

Where the bears climb up swiftly, then look down, awaiting their keeper's instructions.

Where the bats hang upside down, like the heart of a Russian today.

Where the breast of a falcon is like the feathery clouds before a storm.

Where a pheasant folds the golden sunset around it, with all the coals of its fire.

Where, in the face of the tiger, framed with his white beard and with the eyes of an elderly Muslim, we venerate the first follower of the prophet and read the essence of Islam.

Where we begin to think that creeds are the slackening coursing of waves whose motions are species.

And the reason there are so many beasts on earth is that they are able to see god in many different ways.

Where animals which have wearied of howling stand and look at the sky.

Where a seal vividly recalls the torments of sinners, with a wail hurling itself across its cage.

Where comical penguins show the same touching concern for each other as Gogol's bygone landowners.

Garden, Garden, where a beast's gaze means more than chests full of books which have been read.

Garden. Where an eagle is complaining about something, like a child tired of complaining.

Where a husky expends Siberian passion, in performing an ancient ritual of species enmity at the sight of a cat washing itself.

Where goats implore, poking their split hooves through the grill and waving them, eyes acquiring a complacent or joyful expression when they get what they want.

Where a very tall giraffe stands and looks.

Where the midday cannon shot obliges eagles to look at the sky expecting a storm.

Where eagles fall from their high perches, as, during earthquakes, idols fall from temples and the roofs of high buildings.

Where, like a young girl covered by hair, an eagle looks at the sky, then at its claw.

Where we see a tree-creature, in the shape of a deer standing immobile.

Where an eagle perches, turning its neck towards the people and looking at the wall, holding its wings strangely limp. Does it seem to him that he is sailing high above the mountains? Or does he pray? Or is he hot?

Where an elk kisses a flat-horned buffalo through the railing. Where deer lick the cold iron.

Where a black seal jumps along the ground, leaning on its long flippers with the movements of someone tied in a sack, like an iron statue suddenly finding itself seized by fits of uncontrollable merriment.

Where the lion 'Ivanov' with its hairy mane leaps up and strikes the ironwork with his paw when the keeper calls him 'comrade'.

Where lions doze, heads lowered on paws.

Where deer indefatigably knock the rails with their antlers and bang their heads.

Where a particular species of duck in their dry cage raise a unanimous outcry after a brief shower of rain, as if offering thanksgiving to a benefactor – does it have legs and a beak?

Where guinea fowl are at times ladies with ringing voices, with bared and insolent necks and ash-silver bodies, their dresses made to measure by the same tailors who make fittings for starry nights.

Where I refuse to recognize the Malayan bear a fellow northerner and lead a Mongol who is in hiding to the water, and I want to avenge him for Port Arthur.

Where wolves express alertness and devotion with attentively slanted eyes.

Where upon entering a stuffy indoor enclosure where it would be difficult to stay for very long, I am showered with a concerted 'fool, fool!' and seed husks strewn by idle parrots glibly chatting.

Where a fat, gleaming walrus, like a world-weary beauty, waves its slippery black fan-shaped leg and then falls into the water, and when he climbs back onto his platform, on his greasy body appears the moustached, bristling head of Nietszche with his smooth forehead.

Where the jaws of a tall, white, black-eyed llama, and the flat-horned buffalo, and of other ruminants, move evenly to right and left, like the life of a country.

Where the rhinoceros bears in its white and red eyes the inextinguishable rage of a deposed tsar, and alone among beasts does not conceal his contempt for human-beings, as for an uprising of slaves. Within him lurks Ivan the Terrible.

Where seagulls with long and cold, pale blue eyes that seem framed by spectacles, look like international dealers, which we find confirmed by the inborn skill with which on the wing they grab food thrown to the seals.

Where, recalling that Russia honours its great war leaders by calling them 'falcon' and that the eyes of the Cossack, sunk beneath a cleft brow, and those of this bird – issue of the breed of kings – are identical, we begin to understand who taught Russians the military arts. Oh, hawk, piercing the breast of the heron! Oh, its upwardly stretched beak! And the pin, on which too rarely the bearer of honour, loyalty and duty impales insects!

Where a red duck, standing on webbed feet, forces us to remember the skulls of Russians who fell defending their native land, in whose skeletons its forebears wove their nests.

Where the golden tuft of one species of bird contains the fire of the power which is possessed only by those who have vowed celibacy.

Where Russia pronounces the name Cossack, like the screech of an eagle.

Where elephants have forgotten their trumpeting, and make noises as if complaining about disharmony. Perhaps, seeing us only as insignificant beings, they are beginning to discover that insignificant sounds are a sign of good taste. I don't know. Oh, grey, furrowed mountains! Covered with lichen and grass stuck in their crevices!

Where certain resplendent possibilities possessed by beasts are being destroyed, as was inscribed in the great chronicle, The Lay of Igor's Campaign during the burning of Moscow.

1909, 1911

'From resting and sighing'

From resting and sighing,
the festive butterfly
on the prickle of a thistle,
pensive, lights.
A companion flutters
from the rainbow, the glitter,
two silken circles,
gauze threads lacing.
Two early desires,
a column arises,
a meeting assigns,
in the blue deep sinks.
This fragile butterfly
hints at the sword's law.
Ah youngster so young
in a wreath I'll adorn you.
You'll forget the wrong,
you'll forget the treason.

1911–1912

'When horses die – they pant'

When horses die – they pant,
when grasses die – they wither,
when suns die – they fade,
when people die – they sing songs.

1912

'I'm being carried on an elephant's' *

I'm being carried on an elephant's
palanquin – an elephant maidenhazy.
I am loved by all – a new Vishnu,
the litter's wintry phantom interlacing.

You, muscles of this elephant, is not the reason why
you hung about this frame in fabled hunts,
so that so sweetly into the earth
this corpse might limply flow, this tender trunk?

And you, pale phantoms edged in black,
whiter still than cherry white,
feel your stubborn torsos quiver,
supple as the leafy night.

And I, the Bodhisattva, seated on the white elephant,
as ever, fluid and immersed in thought,
as I see this maiden answer me
with the fire of grateful smiles

know that to be a weighty elephant,
has never been devoid of honour.
You maidens, immersed in dream,
be tightly threaded through the palanquin.

The curving tusk's hard to imitate,
as it is to be the widespread foot.
this rite of songs and pipes with laurel wreathes,
we bear him with us, on us, his deep blue eyes.

1913

* 'inspired by an Indian miniature, picturing a form of the god
Vishnu, carried by young maidens. Their interwoven bodies form the
contours of an elephant.'

'Today once more myself I'll hie'

Today once more myself I'll hie
to where there's life's trade, the market,
a brigade of poems I'll deploy
at the market's froth I'll throw down the gauntlet!

1914?

'Years, people and nations'

Years, people and nations
ever flee
like running water
in nature's supple mirror.
The stars are the net, we the fish,
the gods – phantoms in the darkness.

1915

from
Appeal of the Presidents of the Earthly Sphere

Only we, who have rolled *your* three years of war
into the single scroll of a thunderous trumpet,
will sing and shout, shout and sing,
drunk by the delightfulness of the truth
that the Government of the Earthly Sphere
already exists.
It is Us.

Only we have fixed to our brows
the wild garden wreaths worn by the Rulers of the Earthly
    Sphere
inexorable in our bronzed severity,
standing on the rock of the rights we have seized,
raising the banner of time,
we are the bearers of the raw clay of humanity
shaping it into jugs and pitchers of time –
we are the trailblazers in the hunt for human spirits,
and we howl into our grey ocean horns,
hail the human hearts –
Halloo! Who is with us?
Who is our friend and comrade?
Who is with us?
Thus we, the shepherds of the people and humankind
dance and play our bagpipes.
Hey – who will be the greater?
Hey – who will go further?
Only we, standing on the rock
of ourselves and our names,
in the midst of the sea of your bitter pupils
slashed by the hunger of the gallows,
and contorted by the horror of death,
surrounded by the surf of human howling,
will name and in anticipation glorify ourselves
as Presidents of the Earthly Sphere.
What insolence – some will say,
no, they are saints – others will reply.
But we will smile like gods
and point to the sun.
Drag it on a dog's lead,
and hang it on the words –
Liberty, Equality, Fraternity.
Try it at your tribunal of kitchen maids
for the crime that in the antechamber
of this smiling spring
it deposited in us these magnificent thoughts,
these words,
and gave us our angry looks.

It is the guilty one.
We are simply executing the sun's whispered promptings,
when we burst in on you,
as plenipotentiaries, carrying out its instructions,
its strict commandments.
The greasy crowds of humanity
stretch out along the trail
we have made.
London, Paris and Chicago
out of gratitude will change
their names to ours.
But we will forgive them their stupidity.
That of course is in the far distant future,
but meanwhile, mothers
carry off your children,
whenever whatever State appears.
Youths, leap and hide yourselves in caves
and in the depths of the sea,
if you see a State anywhere.
Young girls, and those who can't stand the stench of death,
fall into a faint at the word 'frontiers'.
They smell of corpses.
You know, every execution block was once
a fine fir tree,
or a curly-headed pine.
The block is blackened only because
people are beheaded on it.
It's the same for you, 'State' –
in itself a very good word, as if from a dream –
it contains five sounds,
all very useful and unsoiled.
You grew in the forest of words –
words like ashtray, match, fag-end,
an equal among equals.
But why does the State feed on people?
Why does the Fatherland become a cannibal,
and the Motherland his wife?
Listen!
In the name of all humanity,

we have entered into negotiations
with the states of the past:
If, States, you are as splendid
as you like to describe yourselves,
and as you oblige your servants to describe you,
then why this ambrosia of the gods?
Why do we people crunch in your jaws,
between your canines and your molars?
Listen, States of space,
it is now three years,
that you have given the impression
that humankind is just a pie,
baby food that melts in your mouth:
but what if the rusk jumps up like a razor and says,
'Mummy!'
What if we were to lace it
with poison?
From now on we decree that the words 'By the grace of God'
be changed to 'By the grace of Fiji'.
Can it be seemly for a Lord of the Earthly Sphere –
may his will be done –
to approve of communal cannibalism
taking place within his domain?
And would it not be utter servility
on the part of human beings, as edibles themselves,
to defend their supreme consumer?
Listen! Even ants
squirt acid on a bear's tongue.
We will counter the objection that
a state of space is beyond jurisdiction,
as a collective legal person,
by saying that a human being
is also a two-handed State
made of blood corpuscles, and is also a collective.
If states are bad,
then which one of us will lift a finger
to help prolong their dream,
snuggled in their blanket – for all eternity?

You're not happy by all this, are you, oh, states –
and their governments.
You click your teeth menacingly
and leap about. So what!
We are a higher power
and we will always be ready to reply
to insubordinate states
and their lackeys
with well-aimed writings.
Standing on the deck of the phrase 'star suprastate',
needing no prop in this rocky hour,
we simply put the question, which is the greater –
ourselves, by virtue of our right of insurrection,
our indisputable supremacy,
enjoying the protection of the laws on creative invention,
self-proclaimed Presidents of the Earthly Sphere,
or you – Governments
of the various separate countries of the past,
these unedifying remnants lying around the killing fields
of the two-legged cattle,
in the fluid of whose corpses you are smeared? . . .

21 *April* 1917

The Wind is a Song

The wind is a song.
Of what and of whom?
The sword longs
to become a sphere.
Folk cherish the day of death
like a favourite bloom.
The East now plays, I assure you,
on the strings of the great.

Maybe, the shaman of the gleaming heights
will give us new pride,
and as the throng's guide
I will don the white glacier of mind.

1918–1919

The Proverbs and Tongue-Twisters of Spring

The proverbs and tongue-twisters of spring
crept through the winters' books.
Through deep blue eyes, the keen-eyed one
saw the notes made by the shameworking earth.

Along the arc of the gilded ball
down into the poplar's fishing nets
in these early days the golden coltsfoot
creeps like a golden tortoise.

Spring 1919

from The Procession of the Autumns of Piatigorsk

II

Threatening like a murderer's blade,
as a triple dull razor,
stooped the grey peaks:
here, dead battles dreamed
in the dried blood of a lordly stone.

Beshtau's* crude arc curves,
among rocks scattered more freely than the spoils of war,
like the recording of a far-off sound,
like A or U in a gramophone's groove,
and like the flint arrows
from an ancient hunter's bow.
Full of the spirit of earth, white with cloud,
he menaces with a martial blade the sky,
a fragile throat, soft as flax.
He is a flint knife
in a crude and brutal hand
aimed at the heavens' neck.

But heaven's expanse is not abashed,
the divine brow unfurrowed.
Strong chains like a leper have bound Beshtau,
the supple steppe
has transfixed him to the vale.
Be off, frantic savage!
White eyes float, airy ribbons shift,
in the voice's recording,
in the sound's handwriting
hermits lived.
In the sunlit pines, in the myrtle thicket,
hear robins
and yellow buntings,
inscripted
by the mountain's recording.
See the bright waters and the stone priests,
our fathers maybe prayed to them.

October–November 1921

* BESHTAU: Five Mountains

From ASIA UNCHAINED

'I am hairy with rivers'

I am hairy with rivers . . .
See! The Danube flows along my shoulders,
and this wilful vortex where the Dnieper's rapids grow deep
    blue.
This is Volga falling into my hands,
the comb in my hands is a mountain wall
that combs my hair.
While this long strand
that my fingers hold –
is Amur, where a Japanese girl prays to the sky,
hands folded, at times of storm.

1919

'Asia! I torment myself with you'

Asia! I torment myself with you.
As the brows of a maiden, I comprehend the storm cloud,
as a neck tender with welcome
are your nightly reunions.
Where is he who foretold days of free endearments?
Would that Asia my knees entwine
with the hair of her deep blue rivers
and that the maiden would murmur her secret reproaches,
and silently, joyfully sob,
drying her eyes with the ends of her tress.
The troubled soul of the universe –

she has loved and has suffered
and once more would that feelings be stirred
and warring in the heart
of Makhavira and Zarathustra,
and Savadzha, consumed by the conflict.
I would live through their dying,
give answers and questions,
and you, like a coffer of glittering coins,
would strew your braids at my feet,
whispering, 'Teacher,
together, this day, in truth,
shall we not seek
the paths of greater freedom?'

1920, 1921

Girls That Stride

Girls, the ones, that stride
with the boots of their black eyes
across the flowers of my heart.
Girls, dipping their spears
into the lakes of their lashes.
Girls, bathing their feet
in the lake of my words.

1921

from 'A stream's cold water'

... So we two galloped abreast to the interrogation beneath the
   mountain wall.
And the dry buffalo milk crunched in my mouth,
and afterwards, pure wine in hide flasks, and yellow golden flour.
We flanked the dense forest, where an ancient tree trunk
was so entwined from head to foot in sombre vines
that only the wild boar hurtling like a bullet could graze it.
Sites of camp fires blackened, the ashes white, and bones.
And at times, a thousand herd of sheep, like a flood
led by its shepherd ran to meet us
like the black waves of a living sea.
Suddenly a darkened gorge and the river dark beside us,
and over a thousand stones its pale blue lace,
and all grew dark around, and with a net of fine mist,
with a cape of cold droplets,
we at once were covered. The glowering chasm
of a sudden stood like the stone book of another reader,
open for the eyes of another world.
A mountain hamlet lay strewn, its huts
seemed like the letters of some unknown speech.
There, a red rock rose into the sky,
half a mile high, read by someone before.
But I did not notice the reader in the sky
although it seemed he was nearby,
perhaps enfurled in the rain's turban.
The river foamed in attendance far below,
and scattered trees screened off the heights.
And the stone gazette of the last one hundred thousand years
stood in its uncrumpled splendour.
Are those the traders' shouts? Or reports of passions, veiled and
   tender?
Like the fingers of a hand, the clouds were white above the
   stony news.

Of which large group of centuries
do the lines of stone announcements tell? ...

Summer–Autumn 1921

I and Russia

Russia has given freedom to millions.
A fine deed. It will long be remembered.
so I took off my shirt,
and every mirrorlike skyscraper of my hair,
Every crevice
Of my body's city
hung out its carpets and tapestries
The citizenesses and citizens
of the state of Me
thronged at the windows of the thousand-windowed curls.
Olgas and Igors
of their own free will
rejoiced at the sun, and looked through my skin.
The shirt's dungeon fell away.
But I had simply taken off a shirt –
given the sun to the peoples of Me!
I stood naked by the sea.
Thus I granted freedom to my peoples,
a suntan to the multitudes.

1921

From ZANGEZI

The Deck of Planes of the Word

Mountains. Above a clearing rises a shaggy, vertical rock, like an iron needle under a magnifying glass. Like a staff against a wall, it stands alongside sheer rocky crags, covered with a pine forest. A bridge joins it to the main rock mass, an area formed by a rockslide, looking like a straw hat that had fallen on its head. This space is Zangezi's favourite spot. He is here every morning, reading his poems. From here he delivers his sermons to the people or to the forest A tall fir tree, wildly thrashing its masses of needles in dark blue waves, stands nearby, hiding part of the cliff and seems to have befriended it and safeguards its peace.

At times, the black planes of stone leaves are exposed between its roots. These roots writhe in knots, at the places where the corners of the stone books of a subterranean reader jut out. The singing of the pine forest is carried here. Clumps of deer moss are covered in dew. This path of weeping night.

Living black stones stand among the tree trunks, like the dark bodies of giants going to war.

'I, a butterfly which has flown'

I, a butterfly which has flown
into the living room of human life,
must leave the handwriting of my dust
on its ungrateful windowpanes, a prisoner's signature,
on the strict glass panes of fate.
How stale and grey
the wallpaper of human life!
The windows' transparent 'no'!

I've wiped off my deep blue glow, my speckled patterns,
stilled the blue tempest of my wing, its first flush.
The pollen is removed, my wings have faded, become brittle
    and pellucid.
Wearily I beat against mankind's window.
Eternal numbers are knocking on the other side,
Summoning to their homeland, begging a number to return
    to them.

from Plane XIV

And you, boot-eyed maids,
striding with the greased boots of night
across the sky of my song,
and sowing the money of your eyes
on the public highway!
Tear the viper's sting
from your hissing tresses!
Gaze with the silks of hatred.

from Plane XIX

I hear the call of great cities:
the great gods of sound,
shaking the earth's plate,
have gathered the dust of humanity,
specks of humankind
attentive to their every mouth,
into great cities,
into the lakes of stagnant waves,
into the burial mounds of their thousands.

We breathe a wind into you,
we whistle and sigh,
we sweep the drifts of peoples,
we shake them, and pile them up into the ripples
and measured furrows on the mirror face of centuries.
We give you wars
and the downfall of empires,
we, uncouth sounds,
we, wild horses.
Break us in:
we'll transport you
into other worlds,
keeping faith with the wild rider
of sound . . .
Run like lava, humanity,
saddle steeds of sounds.
Harness the cavalry of sound!

'My skull is a staging post'

My skull is a staging post where words are stored,
boulders of the mind, a concept hoard,
of thoughts now dead a wagon train,
gods of the brow, the bestial tail,
a shipment from fields unknown.
Workers, unload them, as sheaves in laden stacks,
give them space to move, the joy of fleet steps.
See – these seem the brow of intellect,
and these the hymnal of great songs.
Workers, dwellers in the mills of thought,
labour, reap them, set in motion,
give them room to breathe, for their martial flight,
and the fury of conflict and their movement.
And send back to rest at night
disasters and battle.

So that still as the rock of dreams
on maidenlike hay would lie
a rhythmed rank of words
exhausted, and born of Spring.

1921

'In the motherland of glorious death' *

In the motherland of glorious death – on Mashuk,
where the smoke of the martial muzzle
enfurled in its shroud the apocalyptic gaze,
those great and lustrous eyes,
and the pale brow of ample bone,
a troubadour's resplendent eyes,
those temples of effulgent bone –
unto its heaven did the heavens take,
and dead for evermore
is the iron verse soaked in bitterness and anger.
The eagles still remember
the irons' clash,
how the sky rumbled
and the fire flared.
The heavy shell of the cannon's clouds
in the distant heights rolled
their salutation to honour's favourite son.
The son of earth with the eyes of heaven.
And lightning's deep blue fiery branch
gleamed across the sky
and hurled to the tomb's grassy mound
the sky's homage.

* on Lermontov's death

The stormcloud shot in death's salute
shook the leaden crags.
The eyes of the slain minstrel
even to this day undying live
in the misty heights.
And the stormclouds cried, '*Stay your hand,
killers, what are you doing?*' – the heavy voice rolled down.
And to this day, they are prayed to,
those eyes,
in times of storm.
And the lightning streaks
are splendid as those slaughtered eyes.
And the ray of the triple god of death
in fate's mirror
gleamed – the glass of Pushkin, Lensky and their celestial
    brother.
The bard of iron by iron killed.
The flowers of the prophesying soul have withered,
and the muzzle's smoke like a holy father
has intoned the valedictory word,
and the sky has rendered to its dead minstrel
its cloudy tribute.
And to this day in times of storm
the mountain dwellers will say,
'There – see the eyes of Lermontov.'
The sky's hundred mouths gave forth a groan
in martial tribute.
And in the heavens like a vision flamed
the spacious grey-cast eyes.
And to this day, the swift deer live,
and among the clouds they pray
to Russia's writer with the cloud-formed eyes,
when an eagle's flight inscribes on the rocky wall
those great, slow brows.
And since that time, this grey-cast sky
is like the darkened eyes.

October 1921

Hunger

Why are elk and hares leaping through the forest,
making themselves scarce?
People have been eating the bark of poplars,
the green shoots of fir trees . . .
Women and children roam the forest,
gathering birch leaves,
for soup, or broth, or borsh,
tree tops and silver moss –
forest stew.
Children, woodland scavengers,
wander through the thickets,
and bake white worms in the fire,
wild cabbage and fat caterpillars,
or else big spiders, sweeter than nuts.
They catch moles, grey lizards,
with bow and arrow shoot hissing reptiles
and bake pasties of goose-foot.
Out of hunger they chase butterflies
and collect whole sacks of them.
Today there is butterfly borsh –
Mum boils them.
As though in a dream, children
watch a hare tenderly leaping through the trees,
as a vision from a radiant world,
enraptured, they watch with big eyes,
sacred with hunger,
not believing the truth.
But he leaps off, an agile vision,
with blackening ear tips.
An arrow flew in pursuit,
but too late – the ample dinner fled.
The children stand bewitched . . .
'Look there goes a butterfly . . .
Go on, run catch it, the blue one!'
The woods are gloomy, in the distance a wolf approaches

the spot where last year
he had gnawed a lamb.
Like a cub he circled for a long time, sniffed everywhere,
but there was nothing left –
the ants have done their work, just a cloven hoof remains.
Disgruntled, his gnarled ribs pressed together,
he slid back into the forest.
There he'll crush with heavy paw
crimsonbrowed heathcocks and grey wood grouse,
bespattered with flurried snow.
A vixen, a fiery russet ball,
clambered onto a tree stump,
and thought about the future . . .
Really – to become a dog?
To serve humans?
Many nets are spread –
to lie in them
is a dangerous matter.
They will eat a red fox
like they eat dogs!
Dogs no longer bark in the village . . .
The fox began to wash itself with its downy paw,
twisting the fiery sail of its tail upwards.
A squirrel grumbled:
'Where are my nuts and acorns?
The people have eaten them!'
Quietly, transparently, evening came.
With tranquil lisp, a pine kissed a poplar.
Perhaps tomorrow they'll be cut down for breakfast.

7 *October* 1921

'The lice stolidly prayed to me'

The lice stolidly prayed to me,
and each morning crawled over my clothes.
Each morning I executed them –
Listen to the cracking, –
but they appeared again like calm surf.

I devoted my white divine brain
to you, Russia:
be me, be Khlebnikov.
I drove piles into the people's mind, and pivots,
and built a shack on buttresses:
'We – Futurians'.
I did all this as a beggar,
as a thief, everywhere execrated by people.

Autumn 1921

Fragment from What to Do

(AN UNFINISHED POEM)

You saw the blackened hair of Mava,
becoming Volgas of corpses, streams of death.
When I was there, in Petrograd,
with good reason did I in spirit roam over Galicia,
across its mountains high and cold,
prophesying, I voiced the danger from its towers,
and the world war,
the witch-rich dumpling of the war
is Mava's flesh,
that fire hacks and shears,

and smashes order,
and its rear a show of gaudy fascinations,
and its spine, whose bones alone remain
no hide enclothes, while its innards move like stars
in pure concordance with the laws of time . . .

1921–1922

The Solitary Actor

And while, over Tsarskoe Selo
flowed the songs and tears of Akhmatova,
I, uncoiling the skein of the enchantress,
a sleepy corpse, hauled myself across the waste land,
where impossibility was dying,
a weary actor,
headlong striding.
And in the meanwhile, the curly brow
of the subterranean bull in caverns black
champed its bloody human platter
in the smoke of immodest menace.
And robed in the will of the moon
as in a dreaming cloak, the evetide wanderer,
dreaming over chasms leapt
and stepped from rock to rock.
Blind, I walked until
the wind of freedom moved me
and beat me with a slanting rain.
The head of the bull I sheared from powerful meat and bone
and put it near the wall.
As the warrior of truth, I shook it o'er the world:
Look, here it is!
That curly head for which the crowd once had flamed!

And with horror
I saw that by none could I be seen:
that eyes needed to be sown,
that needed was the sower of eyes to stride!

Late 1921–*early* 1922

from The Priest of Flowers' Trumpet

The spring gives the sea
a necklace of dead catfish –
all the beach is strewn with their corpses.
Dogs, seers, prophets,
I, too –
are invited by the sea to a supper
of sleeping fish
on the seashore's tablecloth. Indeed a luxury!
Be human! Don't be shy! Rest, sleep!
Except for the sea, there is no one here.
No one needs my thanks,
sea, you are too great
to wait for me to kiss your hand.
I kiss a wave of the sea as I swim.
The sea lacks the odour of a young lady's tiny hand.
I gathered three pockets of fish roe,
baked them
ate my fill!
Ravens are cawing in the sky!
'Lord, lay to rest' and 'Eternal Memory'
sang the sea
to the foul-smelling dogs.
In this land,
around Pentecost,
time borrows its crimson inks from blood – a friendly loan –

when the tremulous forest is painted
with crimson down.
A tree is impatient, wishes to become
for me, the prophet, a green banner.
But the bloody splashes of Pentecost
are not yet dry.
Its bough's green plumes – a flock of swans –
float in the air,
and the golden ink of spring
is driven back into the sunset in disgrace,
and the forest's crimson
changes to green.
In this land, the dogs don't bark
if you step on a paw at night.
These big dogs
are meek and quiet.
Before falling asleep in its master's hand,
a chick runs up his arm with predatory instinct,
trying to catch midges and mosquitoes.
The tree, O prophet, will serve you as a banner,
the bloody fingers of spring are imprinted on its green leaves . . .

1921, 1922

Notes

THE ZOO GARDEN: Also translated as 'Animal Garden' and 'Bestiary'. Mandelstam wrote a highly anthropomorphized and politicized version in 1916. Boris Pasternak also wrote a poem with the same title more aimed at children. The scholar E.R. Arenzon has pointed out a similarity to 'Songs of Myself' of Walt Whitman, whom Khlebnikov had read, presumably in the Korney Chukovsky translation. There are other poems where Whitman's tone can be felt. This poem was written, according to Khlebnikov's autobiographical prose, on site at the Petersburg Zoo. In a letter to Vyacheslav Ivanov, Khlebnikov writes that while in the zoo he was struck by 'a sort of connection between the camel and Buddhism and the tiger and Islam.'

from APPEAL OF THE PRESIDENTS OF THE EARTHLY SPHERE: Written more in prose than verse and signed also by V. Kamensky and G. Petnikov, then reworked by Khlebnikov.

ZANGEZI: Variants of this name of the hero of the long poem *Zangezi*, which is a combination of the rivers Ganges and Zambezi (as symbols of Eurasia and Africa) include: Zengezi, Mangezi, Changezi, Changili.

IN THE MOTHERLAND OF GLORIOUS DEATH: Written for the 80th anniversary of Mikhail Lermontov's death in a duel; but also undoubtedly highlighting the deaths in August 1921 of Alexander Blok and Nikolay Gumilyov (by firing squad).

HUNGER: Also translated as 'Famine'. There are resonances of Longfellow's *Hiawatha*.

THE SOLITARY ACTOR: The myth of the Minotaur emerges.

THE PRIEST OF FLOWERS' TRUMPET: This is from the long poem 'Tiran without the T'. In Russian and English this indicates Iran, but *Tiran* in Russian means 'tyrant'. Khlebnikov was nicknamed 'comrade priest of flowers' in Iran.

Osip Mandelstam

(2 January 1891–27 December 1938)

Translated by Richard McKane

BORN OF RUSSIAN-SPEAKING Jewish parents in Warsaw (one of
the outposts of the Russian Empire), in January 1891, Osip
Mandelstam is probably the greatest of Russia's many outstanding
twentieth-century poets. He began writing serious poetry in the
heyday of Russian Symbolism in the late 1900s, but made his name
as a member of the small 'Acmeist' group, formally inaugurated in
1913. The group included two other major poets and friends, Anna
Akhmatova and Nikolay Gumilyov. In contrast to the Symbolists'
preoccupation with a mystical 'Higher Reality', the Acmeists' main
focus was man and the individual's place in the challenging, God-
given earthly reality in which he or she is bound to exist. For
Mandelstam in particular, this entailed exploration of his cultural
heritage – at first in a spirit of exuberance, later with a defiant
ethical intensity engendered by the new regime's hostility to the
Christian and humanist tradition with which he identified. For five
years he fell silent, unable to write original verse. Poetry returned
to him in 1930 (*The Moscow Notebooks*, largely unpublishable in his
lifetime). After his first arrest in 1934 for further unpublished lines,
satirical of Stalin, his crowning achievement was *The Voronezh
Notebooks*, composed for posterity in internal exile during 1934–7.
(*The Moscow Notebooks* and *The Voronezh Notebooks* are both
translated by Richard and Elizabeth McKane and published by
Bloodaxe Books.) He was re-arrested in May 1938, and perished in
December, in a prison transit camp outside Vladivostok.

The cycle of 'Poems 1921–5' belong to a period which began
with Mandelstam wandering the south (Kiev, Tiflis, Batum,
Kharkov etc.) in the company of Nadezhda Khazina, whom he
married in spring 1922. After two years in Moscow, they moved in
1924 to Leningrad. Their shiftlessness coincided with a deep psy-
chological crisis in Mandelstam's personal and artistic relation to
the new society – which the intelligentsia to which he proudly

83

belonged had done much to bring about, and on which his material existence now wholly depended. The obsessive preoccupations of the poems are poetry, time, and the state. Their central dilemma is that writing in accordance with conscience and inspiration places the poet at perilous odds with the hungry, 'anti-philological spirit' of the age. Yet society, or 'the age' (latently self-destructive, residually sympathetic), is itself prey to obliteration by a more insatiable predator, time. Paradoxically, the culture which the poet represents might be its one defence; the age's preservation entails the poet's conscious self-immolatory sacrifice. His predicament could be likened to Hamlet's: 'The time is out of joint: – O cursed spite,/ That ever I was born to set it right!' Silence ensued for Mandelstam, in 1925.

The poems are difficult not just because of the issues they treat. They are densely allusive, with complex echoes of many Russian poets, from Derzhavin (1743–1816) and the classicist Batyushkov, through Pushkin and the Romantics (Lermontov, Baratynsky, Tyutchev), the civic poet Nekrasov and his aesthete-contemporary Fet, to early twentieth-century Symbolists (Blok, Annensky and others), Futurists (Mayakovsky, Khlebnikov, Pasternak) and fellow-Acmeists. (Covert references to Gumilyov, executed by the Bolsheviks on trumped-up charges in August 1921, are one of their haunting leitmotifs). The range of reference extends also into Russian prose and far beyond – from Classical Greece and Rome to modern France and Germany. A second and no less formidable difficulty lies in the personal symbolic system which Mandelstam developed at this time: 'fundamental' imagery of salt, stars, birds, fish, food, blood, iron, dryness, etc. 'wanders' from poem to poem, demanding not so much precise allegorical decoding, as an appreciation of expanding contexts and intersecting semantic fields. The underlying poetic logic (which always exists) is startling and sometimes immensely obscure. It generally rests, moreover, on intricate acoustic-semantic associations. To take one simple example, the verb *kolobrodit*, 'to play games', at the end of 'A chill tickles', anticipates *kolobok*, the bread roll in the next poem, 'How the leaven . . . '. The two are interconnected, and co-related to the theme of 'poet'. The poems literally abound in all manner of such paronomastic links and interpretative indices.

Inevitably, the notes do no more than skim the surface, offering skeletal observations by way of rudimentary commentary. They are much indebted to previous scholars, and particularly to the work of Omry Ronen, the leading specialist on the verse of these years. In many ways, however, the most illuminating background to the poems are Mandelstam's own essays and autobiographical prose: the extracts quoted in the notes are my own translation. Readers wishing for a general introduction to Mandelstam might still turn to Clarence Brown's pioneering book (CUP, 1973); while the seminal account of his life, especially of the harrowing later years, is the profoundly moving memoirs of his faithful wife and widow, Nadezhda (*Hope Against Hope; Hope Abandoned*).

Michael Basker

Concert in the Railway Station

Impossible to breathe, and the firmament teems with worms,
and not a single star speaks out,
but God sees: there is music above us.
The station trembles from the singing of the Muses,
and rent apart by the steam engines' whistles
the air of violins is fused together once more.

A huge park. The glass globe of the station.
The iron world is bewitched again.
The coach rushes solemnly
to the eloquent feast, to misty Elysium.
Cry of the peacock, thunder of the piano –
I am too late. I'm afraid. This is a dream.

And I enter into the glass forest of the station.
The violins' structure is in tears of confusion.
The chorus of the night starts off wildly.
There's a scent of roses in rotting glasshouses
where a familiar shadow spent the night
under the glass sky in the nomad hordes.

It seems to me that the iron world
is all in music and foam, trembling so wretchedly.
I press my face against the glass of the porch:
the hot steam blinds the pupils of the bows.
Where are you going? For the last time the music
plays to us at the funeral feast for the dear shadow.

1921

'I was washing outside at night'

I was washing outside at night –
the firmament shone with coarse stars.
Beam of a star, like salt on an axe,
the full barrel freezing.

The gates are locked
and the earth in all conscience is so stern:
I doubt if one could ever find a base
purer than the truth of fresh canvas.

Like salt a star thaws in the barrel
and the ice-cold water is blacker,
death purer, trouble more saline
and the world more honest, more terrible.

1921

'For some winter is arack and blue-eyed punch'

For some winter is arack and blue-eyed punch,
for some, wine cup fragrant with cinnamon,
for others, it is given to bring into the smoky hut
the salty orders of the cruel stars.

A few warm chicken droppings
and the muddle-headed sheep warmth;
I'll give everything for life, I'm so in need of caring
and a sulphur match could warm me.

Look: in my hand there is just an earthenware pot
and the chirping of the stars tickles my feeble hearing,

but one cannot help liking the yellow of the grass
and the warmth of the soil through the pathetic hay dust.

To quietly stroke the cow-hair and turn the straw,
to be hungry like an apple tree, protected with sacking in winter,
and stretch out to a stranger tenderly, senselessly,
and to circle in the emptiness and wait patiently.

Let the conspirators hasten through the snow
like a flock of sheep, and the fragile snow-crust creak,
for some winter is wormwood and acrid smoke before a night's
    rest,
for others the vertiginous salt of solemn injuries.

Oh, if only I could carry a lantern on a long pole
and with a dog out in front under the salt of the stars
come to the yard of the fortune-teller with a cockerel in the pot.
But the white, white snow eats the eyes till they ache.

1922

'The bull violently ploughs the green waves'

The bull violently ploughs the green waves
with pink foam of exhaustion on its soft lips.
It snorts, does not like rowing – a ladies' man,
not used to the burden on his back and this great labour.

Occasionally the wheeling dolphin leaps out
and the spiky sea-urchin is glimpsed.
Take everything, tender hands of Europa –
where will you find a more desirable yoke to restrain the neck?

Europa listens bitterly to the powerful splash of waves,
the fattened sea seethes like a spring.
The oily sparkle of the waters terrifies her
and she would like to slide off the rough flanks.

How much more dear to her are the squeaking rowlocks,
the breast of the broad deck, the flocks of sheep
and the flashing of fish by the high prow.
The oarless rower carries her further.

1922

'A chill tickles the crown of the head'

A chill tickles the crown of the head
though I don't admit it immediately,
and time cuts me down as though
it shaved off the heel from your shoe.

Life overpowers itself,
the sound melts gradually,
there is always something missing,
never quite the time to remember something.

But it was better before
and of course you cannot compare
how the blood stirs now
and how it stirred before.

You see the movement of lips
will not pass in vain,
and the crown plays games
though it's condemned to be cut down.

1922

'How the leaven of loaves rises'

How the leaven of loaves rises
and how good it is at first,
and the good-housewifely soul
is crazed with the heat.

The domes puff out round
with the heat
like bread St Sophias
on a cherubim table.

Time, the royal herdsboy,
grabs words like little rolls,
to coax out the wondrous extra bake,
both strongly and fondly.

The stale stepchild, outcast of the ages,
finds its place – drying off
among the loaves
that have already been taken out of the oven.

1922

'I cannot know'

I cannot know
when this song began –
isn't a thief rustling to its tune,
or a mosquito prince singing it?

I wanted to speak again
about nothing at all,
to strike like a match, to nudge
the night with a shoulder to wake it.

To raise like a choking haystack
the air that torments one like a hat.
To unsew and shake out the sack
that contains the caraway seeds

so that the knot of the rose-coloured blood,
the ringing of these dry grasses,
could be found stolen
through the age, the hayloft, dream-sleep.

1922

'I leaned a short ladder'

I leaned a short ladder
against the tousled haystack and climbed.
I breathed in the hay-dust of milky stars
and breathed in the matted hair of space.

I thought a while: why wake
the swarm of elongated sounds
in order to catch the miraculous harmony
of Aeolus in this eternal squabble?

There are seven stars in the plough of the Great Bear.
There are five good senses on earth.
The darkness swells and rings
and swells and rings again.

The huge unharnessed cart
sticks up across the universe.
The ancient chaos of the haystack
starts tickling and gives off dust . . .

We don't rustle our own scales,
we sing against the nap of the world,
we make the lyre as though we are hurrying
to grow a rough fleece.

The mowers bring back
the goldfinches from the fallen nests,
I tear myself from the burning ranks
and will return to the familiar series of sounds.

So the connection of pink blood
and the dry-handed ring of the grass
should make a final farewell: one getting firmer
while the other becomes a futurist dream.

1922

'The wind brought us comfort'

The wind brought us comfort
and we sense the dragonflies'
Assyrian wings in the azure sky,
the re-formation of the jointed darkness.

The lower layer of the darkened skies
was dark with the storm of war,
with a micaceous, membraned forest
of six-armed, flying bodies.

There is a blind corner in the blue sky
and a fateful star always trembles
in the blissful middays
like a hint of the clotted night.

Azrael, the angel of death
with crippled scaly wings, forces on
against all odds, and with his lofty arm
protects the conquered firmament.

1922

The Soft Moscow Rain

It shares so stingily
its sparrow cold –
a little for us, a little for the clumps of trees,
a little for the cherries for the hawker's stall.

And a bubbling grows in the darkness,
the light fussing of tea-leaves,
as though an ant-hill in the air
were feasting in the dark green grass;

fresh drops stirred
like grapes in the grass,
as though the hot-bed of the cold
was revealed in web-footed Moscow.

1922

The Age

My age, my beast, who will have the strength
to look into your pupils
and glue with his blood
the backbone of two centuries?
Blood-the-builder gushes from
the throat of worldly things.
The parasite just trembles
on the threshold of new days.

While life lasts, a creature
must bear his spine,
and the wave plays
with an unseen backbone.
Again the crown of life has been brought
like a lamb to sacrifice.
The infant age of the earth
is like a child's tender cartilage.

In order to tear the age out of captivity,
in order to start a new world,
one must bind the joints
of the knotty days with a flute.
This is the age rocking the wave
with human anguish,
and an adder in the grass breathes
the golden measure of the age.

The buds will burst again,
the green shoot will spurt,
but your backbone is smashed
my beautiful, pitiful age,
and with a senseless smile
you look back, weak and cruel,
like a beast, once supple,
at the tracks of his own paws.

1922

The Finder of the Horseshoe

(A Pindaric fragment)

We look at the forest and say:
here is the timber for ships and masts,
pink pines,
to their very peaks free from any furry burden;
they will screech in the storm
like lonely Italian pines
in the enraged forestless air.
The vertical will be maintained under the wind's salty heel,
riveted to the dancing deck.

And the seafarer in his unbridled thirst for space
carries his frail sextant with him over the furrowed sea
and will compare the rugged surface of the seas
and the gravity of the bosom of the earth.

Let us say,
as we breathe in the smell
of tears of resin oozing through the ship's timbers,
admiring the boards,
bolted, shaped nicely into bulkheads –
not by the peaceful carpenter of Bethlehem, but by another,
the father of journeys, the friend of the seafarer:
they stood on the earth,
uncomfortable as the spine of an ass,
summits forgetful of roots.
They rustled on a famous mountain ridge
under the fresh torrents of rain
and proposed unsuccessfully to the sky
that it exchange their noble burden for a pinch of salt.

Where to begin?
Everything creaks and rocks.
The air quivers with comparisons.
No one word is better than another.
The world buzzes with metaphors.

Light two-wheeled carts,
harnessed garishly to dense flocks of straining birds,
fall apart
rivalling the snorting favourites of the hippodromes.

Thrice blest is he who gives a song a name:
a song decorated with a title
lives longer than others.
It is marked out from its friends by a band round the forehead
which heals forgetfulness and the overpowering stupefying
    stench –
be it the proximity of a man
or the smell of a strong beast's fur
or simply the scent of thyme rubbed between palms.
Air can be dark as water and everything alive in it swims like
    a fish
forcing aside with its fins a sphere
dense, resilient, warmish,
a crystal in which wheels turn and horses shy,
the moist black earth of Neaira, ploughed anew every night
with tridents, mattocks and ploughs.
The air is kneaded just as stickily as the earth:
one can never get out of it, and it's difficult to get into.

A rustle runs round the trees like a green game of rounders.
The children are playing knucklebones with the vertebrae
    of dead animals.
The fragile chronology of our age is coming to an end.
Thanks for the past:
it was me who was at fault, I went wrong. I lost count.
The age was ringing like a golden ball,
hollow, cast, unsupported by anyone,
answering 'yes' and 'no' to the slightest touch.
This is how a child answers:
'I'll give you an apple', or 'I won't give you an apple'.
And his face is an exact mould of the voice which pronounces
    these words.

The sound is still ringing although the cause of the sound has
    disappeared.
The horse lies in the dust and snorts in its lather,
but the steep curve of its neck
still retains the memory of the race with outflung legs
when the legs didn't number four
but, renewed in four relays,
they were as many as the stones on the road,
as many as the thrusts off the earth of the fiery, fevered steed.

So,
the finder of the horseshoe
blows the dust off it
and rubs it with wool till it shines,
then
he hangs it over the threshold
to let it rest
and it no longer has to strike sparks from flint.

Human lips
    which have no more to say
retain the shape of the last word they spoke,
and the arm still feels the weight
although the pitcher
    is half empty from splashing
        while being carried home.

It is not I who am saying what I am saying now:
it is something dug up from the earth, like grains of fossilized
    wheat.

Some
    stamp a lion on coins,
others –
    a head;
Miscellaneous artefacts of copper, gold and bronze
lie in the ground with equal honours.
The age tried to bite through them and its teeth came out.

Time stamps on me like a coin
and I am lost.

Moscow, 1923

Slate Ode

We will only understand from the voice
what was scratched there, what was fought for there . . .

Star with star – a powerful meeting-point,
the flinty road from the old song,
the language of flint and air,
flint with water, ring with horseshoe.
A milky, slate-pencil drawing
on the soft slate of the clouds –
not the learning of worlds
but the delirium of the half-sleep of sheep.

We sleep standing in the thick night
under a warm sheepskin hat.
The spring burbles back to the well enclosure
in a little chain, warbling, speaking.
Here terror writes, here shifts write
with a milky lead pencil.
Here matures the rough draft
of the disciples of running water.

The mountain goat cities,
the powerful stratification of flints;
yet one more ridge
and there are the sheep churches and settlements!
The plumb line preaches to them,
water teaches them, time sharpens them
and the transparent forest of the air
is long saturated with all things.

The motley day is swept away with shame
like a hornet dead by the honeycomb.
Night-the-vulture carries
the burning chalk and feeds the slate.
O, to wipe the impressions of day
off the iconoclastic blackboard
and to shake off already transparent visions
like tossing out a fledgling.

The fruit almost burst. The grapes were ripe.
The day raged as days rage.
A friendly game of knucklebones was played.
The vicious sheepdogs wore their fur coats even at midday.
Like débris from the icy heights –
the seamy side of greenness –
the hungry water flows,
whirling, playing, a young beast.

And as a spider crawls towards me –
where every meeting-point is splashed by the moon –
I hear the squeaks of slate
at a stunning steepness.
I break the night, the burning chalk
for a firm momentary entry,
I change sound into the singing of arrows,
I change form into an angry bustard.

Who am I? Not an honest stone-mason,
not a tiler, not a shipwright:
I'm a double-dealer, with a double soul.
I am the friend of night, the skirmisher of day.
Blessèd is he who called flint
the disciple of running water.
Blessèd is he who fastened a strap
round the soles of the mountains on firm earth.
Now I study the diary
of the scratches of the slate summer,
the language of flint and air

with a stratum of darkness and a stratum of light,
and I want to put my fingers
into the flint road of the old song
as into the wound, to conclude the meeting:
flint with water, ring with horseshoe.

1923, 1937

Paris

I understand cobblestones' language more than that of doves.
Here the stones are doves, the houses like dovecotes,
and the tale of horses' hoofs flows in a bright little stream
along the loud pavements of the great-grandmother of cities.

Here the childlike crowds, spongers off events,
frightened flocks of Parisian sparrows
hastily pecked the oatmeal of lead crumbs,
peas scattered by a Phrygian grandmum,
forgotten currants float in the air
and the wicker basket remains in the memory
and the close-set houses stand like twins,
like a row of milk teeth, in an old person's gums.

Months were given nicknames here like kittens
and they gave milk and blood to the tender lion cubs,
but if they grew up – could their big heads remain
on their shoulders for even a year or two?
With big heads, they raised their hands
and played with oaths on the sand like apples at a picnic.
I find it hard to speak: I did not witness anything
but nevertheless I will say: I remember one
who lifted his paw like a fiery rose
and like a child showed everyone the thorn in the flesh.
No one listened to him; the coachmen laughed

and the children gnawed at apples, while the barrel-organ
    played.
They stuck up posters, made ambushes,
they sang songs, roasted chestnuts,
and the horses flew from the dense greenery
down the bright street as though it were a cutting in a forest.

1923

The Sky is Pregnant with the Future

Once more the cacophony of war
on the ancient plateaux of the world,
and the propeller's blade glistens
like the sharpened bone of a tapir.
The equation of the wing and death,
having flown from the feasts
of algebra, remembers the measure
of other ebony toys,
the hostile night, the enemy breeding-ground
of short creatures, web-footed,
and the young force of gravity:
here began the power of the few.

So, prepare to live in the time
where there is no wolf, no tapir
and the heavens are pregnant with the future –
with the wheat of the sated ether.
For today the conquerors
went round the cemeteries of flight,
they broke the dragonfly wings
and executed with little hammers.
Let's listen to the sermon of thunder
like the grandchildren of Sebastian Bach,
and let us place organ wings

in the east and in the west!
Let's throw the apple of the storm
onto the table for the feasting earthlings
and let us place on a glass dish
a cloud in the middle of victuals.

Let's cover all anew
with the damasked tablecloth of space,
talking things through, rejoicing,
giving food one to the other.
At the round Court of Peace
the blood will turn to ice at dawn,
in the deep, pregnant future
a huge honey-bee is buzzing.

And you, flying in timelessness
under the whip of war, for the power of the few –
if you only had the honour of mammals,
if you only had the conscience of the flipper-footed!
And the more sad, the more bitter it is for us
that bird-people are worse than beasts
and that unwillingly we have more trust in
carrion-crows and kites.
Like a hat of Alpine cold,
year in and year out, in the heat and summer
the cold palms of war
are on the high forehead of humanity.
And you, deep and sated,
having become pregnant with the azure,
scaled, many-eyed,
the alpha and omega of the storm,
to you – alien and eyebrowless –
from generation to generation
always a lofty and new
surprise is communicated.

1923, 1929

'Like a tiny little body with its wing'

Like a tiny little body with its wing
turned, brimming over to the sun,
the incendiary glass
caught fire across the empyrean.

As the mosquito trifle
whined and rang in the zenith,
to the quiet singing of ground-beetles
the splinter agonized in the azure:

'Don't forget me: execute me,
but give me a name, give me a name:
understand me, it'll be easier for me with it,
in the pregnant, deep blue.'

1923

1 January 1924

He who has kissed time's exhausted forehead
will remember afterwards with a son's love
how time lay down to sleep
in a snowdrift of wheat outside the window.
He who has opened his sickly eyelids to the age,
revealing two big sleepy eyeballs,
will for ever hear the noise
of the roaring rivers of the deceptive and sombre times.

The tyrant age has two sleepy eyeballs
and a beautiful clay mouth,
but as it dies it will fall upon
the numb arm of its ageing son.
I know that life breathes more weakly every day.
In a while they'll cut short
the simple song about injuries of clay
and pour the tin mask over the lips.

O life of clay! O the dying of the age!
I am afraid that the only person to understand you
will be a man with a helpless smile
of one who has lost himself.
What agony! To search for a lost word,
to raise sick eyelids
and with lime in the blood
to gather night herbs for an alien generation.

The age. A layer of lime hardens in the blood
of the sick son. Moscow sleeps sound as a wooden chest
and there is nowhere to run from the tyrant age . . .
The snow smells of apples as of old.
I want to run from my own home.
But where to? It's dark outside
and my conscience looms white before me,
like salt being spread on a paved road.

I get myself together to go a short distance
through the backstreets, past the starling boxes and thatched
        eaves,
an ordinary traveller in a flimsy coat
struggling to button up the sleigh rug.
Street after street flashes past
and the frosty sound of the sleigh is crunchy like an apple,
and the loop is tight, won't give
and keeps slipping out my hands.
The winter night crashes through the streets of Moscow
as though it were ironmongery.

It thuds like a frozen fish, then lashes with steam
from rosy cafés, like the silver scales of a roach.
Moscow, Moscow again. I say to her 'Hello!
Don't be too harsh! It's still just about all right.
I respect the brotherhood of harsh
frost and the pike justice as of old.

The chemist's red sign flares in the snow.
There's a typewriter clicking somewhere.
I see the sleigh driver's back and the foot-deep snow:
what else do you want? They won't touch you. They won't
    kill you.
Winter is a beautiful woman, and the Capricorn sky
is strewn with stars, burning with milk,
and the horse-hair sleigh-rug is rubbing
and tinkling against the frozen runners.

The backstreets were smoking like a kerosene stove
and were swallowing the snow, the ice, the red sign.
All peels before them in a little Soviet sonatina
looking back at 1920.
Once more the snow smells of apples.
Will I betray to evil, shaming talk
my wonderful oath to the Fourth Estate
and promises weighty as teardrops?

Who else will you kill? Who else will you praise?
What lies will you invent?
A typewriter clicks: quick, tear out the keys
and you'll find the carcass of a pike.
The layer of lime in the blood of the sick son
will melt away, blessèd laughter will break out
but the simple sonatina of the typewriters
is just a shadow of those more powerful sonatas.

1924

'No, never was I anyone's contemporary'

No, never was I anyone's contemporary,
such an honour does not suit me.
Oh, how offensive is any other bearer of my name,
it was not me, it was someone else.

The tyrant age has two sleepy eyeballs
and a beautiful clay mouth,
but as it dies it will fall upon
the numb arm of its ageing son.

I raised sick eyelids with the age –
two big sleepy eyeballs,
the thundering rivers told me
of the progress of peoples' inflamed rivalries.

One hundred years ago the camp bed
was white with pillows
and the clay body stretched out strangely –
the first intoxication of the century was ending.

What a light bed
among the creaking world campaign!
Well then, if we can't forge another,
let's age with the age.

In a hot room, in a hooded sledge, in a tent,
the century is dying, and then:
two sleepy eyeballs on the wafer of the cornea
gleam with a feather-like flame.

1924

'You, low houses'

You, low houses
with square windows –
welcome, welcome
mild St Petersburg winter.

Unfrozen skating rinks are displayed
like the ribs of a pike
and the skates still lie
in a heap in the blind halls.

For how long did the potter
sail up and down the canal
with his red-glazed ware,
selling his honest goods by the granite steps?

Boots walk, grey boots
by the Gostiny Arcade
and mandarin oranges
peel themselves.

Roast coffee in a packet,
straight home from the cold,
golden mocha ground
by an electric mill.

Low, chocolate,
brick houses.
Welcome, welcome,
mild St Petersburg winter.

Waiting rooms with pianos
where doctors provide their patients
with armchairs and piles
of old literary magazines.

After a visit to the baths or the opera
it does not matter where one goes.
That indefinable, last
warm tram feeling . . .

1924

'This night, in all honesty'

This night, in all honesty,
I was walking, up to my waist in snow,
from a station halt that I did not know.
I saw a hut, went in and watched from the doorway,
monks drinking tea with salt
and a gypsy girl toying with them.

The gypsy girl kept gesturing
with her eyebrows by a bedhead.
Her words were pitiful:
she sat there till dawn
and said: 'Give me
a shawl, anything, a ragged shawl.'

You can never get back the past,
the oak table, the knife in the salt cellar
and the big-bellied hedgehog instead of the loaf;
they wanted to sing, and couldn't,
they wanted to get up – and went out through the window
in an arc into the hunchbacked yard.

Half an hour passes
and the horses are crunching and chewing
black oats by the bucketful.
The gates squeak at dawn
and they harness up in the yard.
Hands slowly get warm.

The threads are pulled from twilight's canvas.
Chalk diluted with water,
though to no avail boredom spills
and through the transparent peasant picture
the milky day looks in at the window
and a scrofulous rook flies past.

1925

'Life fell like a *coup de foudre*'

Life fell like a *coup de foudre*,
like an eyelash into a glass of water,
having lied to the root,
I blame no one . . .

Do you want an apple of the night,
some spicy drink, fresh, sharp.
If you wish I'll pull off your boots
and lift them like a feather.

An angel in a bright web
stands in a golden sheepskin,
the rays of light of the street lamp
reflect upon his tall shoulders.

But perhaps a cat could be startled,
turn into a wild hare
and suddenly stitch across the path
disappearing into somewhere.

How the crimson of your lips trembled,
how you gave your son tea,
spoke random words
about nothing, aimlessly.

Unexpectedly you stuttered over words
became a liar, smiled
so that your features flashed
with clumsy beauty.

There is a country beyond eyelashes,
beyond the palace cowl
and the seething garden –
there you'll be my wife.

Having picked dry pairs of boots
and golden sheepskins,
hand in hand, the two of us
will walk down the same street,

without backward looks, without impediment
to the shining landmarks
and the street lamps are flooded with light
from sunset to dawn.

1925

'I will rush through the gypsy camp'

I will rush through the gypsy camp of the dark street
searching for a cherry laurel branch in a black, sprung carriage,
for a hood of snow, for the eternal, milling sound.

I only remembered the misfirings of chestnut locks,
slightly smoky with bitterness, or rather formic acid;
they leave an amber dryness on the lips.

At such moments the whole atmosphere seems to me to be
    hazel
and the rings of pupils are clothed in bright surrounds
and I know about apple-pink skin . . .

And yet the runners of the coachman's sleigh squeaked,
barbed stars looked piercingly through the weave of the
    coarse rug
and the hoofs beat out bold on the frozen keys.

But the only light is from the barbed untruth of the stars.
Life will swim past like the surf of a theatrical hood
and there is no one to whom you can say: 'through the gypsy
    camp of the dark street' . . .

1925

Notes

by Michael Basker

CONCERT IN THE RAILWAY STATION: The opening poem of the cycle combines childhood memories of concerts at the Pavlovsk Station outside St Petersburg in the mid-1890s ('... a sort of Elysium. Engine whistles and railway bells mingled with the patriotic cacophony of the *1812 Overture* ... The dampish air of mouldering parks, the smell of rotting flowerbeds and hothouse roses, mingling with the heavy emanations of the buffet') with multiple allusions to nineteenth- and early twentieth-century authors, from Delvig, through Gogol and Tyutchev to Blok and Annensky – the Acmeists' 'teacher' who died on a station platform in 1909. The poem is an elegy for Annensky, and for pre-revolutionary poetry and culture, its components now fragmented and cataclysmically distorted (Lermontov's famous 'star speaks with star' becomes 'not a single star speaks out', etc.). This was an age of 'iron' and 'music', for which the glass-plated Pavlovsk station – Russia's first – is a fitting symbol (the Russian for station – *vokzal* – once also signified 'concert', after London's Vauxhall Gardens); but in another respect, the 'music' of the past is at odds with the 'iron' of the present, and each is fatally weakened. The old world is no longer supportive of life, and the poet seems doomed to exist in (or journey into) an alien realm, of mechanical movement, devoid of spiritual coherence.

'I WAS WASHING OUTSIDE AT NIGHT': Written in Tiflis in autumn 1921, in response to news of Nikolay Gumilyov's execution by the Bolsheviks – and to Anna Akhmatova's poetic reaction to that event in 'Terror, rummaging through things in the dark'. The washing suggests rituals of purification, as preparation for new life – or death. Its outcome, in the words of the leading authority on Mandelstam's verse of this period, Omri Ronen, is 'a cosmic sense of supreme awareness, attained as the tragic earthly reality of disaster and death is intensified to the level of a fearsome and purifying self-sacrifice'. The eternal clarity and truth of the stars, now melting in the barrel, contrasts the surrounding darkness, while salt, another recurrent image of the poems, appears to connote the (Russian) poet's painful, sorrowing acceptance of moral obligation: a covenant with God (cf. Leviticus 2:13, Numbers 18:19, Mark 9:49–50), entailing austere fidelity to creative life, leading to inevitable sacrificial death.

'FOR SOME WINTER IS ARACK': A companion piece to the preceding poem, regarded by the critic A. Parnis as a pre-emptive elegy to Khlebnikov. Commentary is provided by Mandelstam's recollection of an old woman, living 'in a festive cleanliness, anticipating death', from whom he rented a room in a wattle hut in Feodosiya in 1919–20: she 'kept her lodger like a bird, believing that he must have his water changed, his cage cleaned, seed fed to him. At that time it was better to be a bird than a man, and the temptation to become the old woman's bird was great ... If you went outside on one of those icy Crimean nights and listened to the sound of steps on the snowless clay earth, ... if you took a gulp of this brew of muted life, thickened on the viscous bark of dogs and salted with stars, a sense of the plague descended upon the world became physically clear, the Thirty Years' War, with pestilential sores, dimmed lights, barking dogs and frightened silence in the homes of little people.' Though the occult portents brought into the hut remain unread, salt and snow again connote the purifying, sacrificial pain of conscience, and the need to base poetic destiny on personal moral integrity cannot be ignored. In part, perhaps, the poem is a rejection of the easy path of emigration. Arack is grape vodka.

'THE BULL VIOLENTLY PLOUGHS': Inspired by the painter V.A. Serov's version of the 'Rape of Europa', the poem reflects Mandelstam's conception of contemporary Europe as an enormous storage barn of human wheat-grain – grain which longs to be ground and baked into bread, signifying the restitution of individuals into a new, non-mechanistic nationhood. In present disarray, each grain merely preserves the mythical memory of Jupiter who 'turned himself into a simple bull' and laboured to exhaustion in order to 'carry across the waters of the earth a precious burden, tender Europa' ('The Wheat of Humanity'). There is eroticism alongside this guarded optimism: and the poet also expresses pity for his wife as Europa, borne away from the comfortable 'ordinary' life she yearned for by, in her words, a 'feckless wanderer, who carries her to destinations unknown'.

'A CHILL TICKLES THE CROWN OF THE HEAD': Addressed to the poet's wife. The movement of lips is one of Mandelstam's recurrent metaphors for poetic creativity. The first line, according to Viktor Krivulin, is indicative of Mandelstam's premature balding.

'HOW THE LEAVEN OF LOAVES RISES': On the imagery of bread, see note to 'The bull violently'. Here there are strong eucharistic connotations, and the spiritual bread is also connected to poetry ('words like little rolls') and the poet (the 'stale stepchild ... '). The Russian *kolobok* is specifically a 'little roll' made from left-overs, scraped off the surfaces on which the dough was prepared. In Russian fairy-tale, the baked *kolobok* sings songs to avoid being eaten by various animals, but fails to trick the wily, predatory fox, which gulps it down.

'I CANNOT KNOW': The first of two closely related pieces, in which a haystack at night is the background to meditations on poetry. It examines the bond of the poet's life with his poetry, and their linkage with past and future. The basic 'plot' initiates a dialogue with the poetry of Fet ('On a stack of hay in a southern night'); the 'mosquito prince', probably signifying poetry and poet, derives from Derzhavin. The imagery of stanzas 2 and 3 variously suggests the urge to create; even the sack of caraway seeds – with a possible echo of Gumilyov – seems to be an analogue of poetry. The knot (bond, tie) of blood perhaps signifies the poet's personality and physicality as well as his 'blood connection' with other generations. The dry grasses (cf. hay, etc.) are presumably his poems; and the final image must be understood in the light of his view that true poetry is 'stolen' (cf. the 'thief' in line 3) from eternity, the air, the age. His hope is that his poetry be preserved and 'found' again in a future age.

'I LEANED A SHORT LADDER': The haystack becomes more menacing, and the poet questions the necessity for poetry in a world where truths seem simple. But poetic themes 'swell' irrespective of the poet's will; and he creates in 'eternal squabble' with the 'ancient chaos' of the universe, and the asphyxiating disarray of the apocalyptic present. Isolation (the 'rough fleece') and, again, death (the goldfinches) are the price of creative defiance; and in the last stanza, the previous poem's pledge of continuity seems lost. Life may be suppressed, and poetry may assume a new form, a futuristic 'transrationalism' which may or may not be equated with Mandelstam's own shifting idiom. Stanza 4 may relate to Bosch's painting of 'The Haywain'.

'THE WIND BROUGHT US COMFORT': The poem recalls the First World War and the years immediately preceding it. The 'we' are perhaps primarily Acmeist poets, and there is a polemic with Blok's Symbolist perceptions of 'azure sky' as a portent of spiritual transformation. The membraneous dragonfly-aeroplane wings evoke those of Assyrian human-headed bulls; another key to interpretation is Mandelstam's essay on 'The Nineteenth Century', which he regarded as an age of now-outmoded relativism, understanding and polymorphousness. The twentieth century, by contrast, 'opens under the sign of magisterial intolerance, exclusivity and conscious incomprehension of other worlds. In the veins of our century flows the heavy blood of extremely distant, monumental cultures, perhaps Egyptian and Assyrian.' Azrael is the Judaic embodiment of evil, and Islamic angel of death.

THE SOFT MOSCOW RAIN: Cf. Mandelstam's prose sketch 'A Cold Summer': '[It seemed] as though a sack of ice which just wouldn't melt was hidden in the thick greenery of Neskuchnyi Gardens, and coldness crawled out across the whole of web-footed Moscow'. The tea-leaves convey the impression of birds in the sky; the ant-hill as an image of the populous city has its earliest Russian precedent in Dostoevsky.

THE AGE: The double question of the opening lines finds tentative (and familiar) response in stanza 3: it is the sacrificial blood of the comprehending artist which might heal the disjointed age and so re-establish broken continuity between past and future; perhaps, as Mandelstam wrote in 'The Nineteenth Century', which might 'europeanize and humanize the twentieth'. The 'backbone of two centuries', however, evidently refers to the fractured vertebrae of the two hundred years since Peter the Great: the once vigorous age now in ruin. The flute, with overtones of Masonic construction, evokes the contemporary poet Mayakovsky (author of *The Backbone Flute*, lyricist now turned poet-of-revolution) and, in connection with 'tearing out of captivity', the archetypal poet Orpheus. The 'backbone flute' is the artist as well as his instrument, and, his integrity perhaps compromised, the painful task of engendering 'new' harmony may prove impossible. Thus the 'wave' – of history or nature? – toys with the fragmented present, and stanza 2 shows the death rather than birth of a child (the futile sacrifice of the young, revolutionary era?). A snake lurks ominously in the grass (an adder killed Eurydice, whom Orpheus failed to restore to life); and in stanza 4 nature thrives while the human age – and perhaps especially the 'beautiful, pitiful' Russian intelligentsia, looking regretfully back over its tragic post-Petrine path – is crippled and moribund. The past, a once cruel beast, is scarcely worthy to be mourned; and 'parasitic trembling' at the threshold of the new characterizes the present and possibly its artist-intellectual. The golden age promises to elude future realization.

THE FINDER OF THE HORSESHOE: Mandelstam's longest single poem, and the only one in (significantly fragmented) free verse. Originally subtitled 'A Pindaric Fragment', this is another meditation on history, art and the poet, the complex ambiguities of which, revolving around concepts of cyclical progression and return or chaotic dissolution, seem to convey deepening despair. The American scholar Clare Cavanagh explains: 'The horseshoe is all that remains of the great odic tradition that had its beginnings in the chariot races that were Greece's most prestigious competitions. And the horseshoe finder himself, the latter-day poet who stumbles on this memento of past greatness, can answer a fragment only with a fragment. He marks the passing of an entire civilization, the civilization that began with Pindar and the other great poets of ancient Greece and that may be ending with him, unworthy scion of a mighty culture.'

The trees of the opening become a ship which is that of state and of poetry; the seafarer is both poet-Odysseus, and head of state: Peter I or Lenin. In section 3 this commonality is sundered and poetry, forgetful of its roots, falters. The 'band round the forehead' may denote Mnemosyne – goddess of memory and mother of the Muses – and hence the survival of a poetry of 'names'; but it may also suggest, via Pindar, a patron – hence the 'name' of a political protector the poet does not have, and he plunges into threatening delirium. For Mandelstam the ploughing of the 'black earth' of time was a metaphor for creating poetry; but inappropriate, impersonal implements, perhaps emblematic of the Workers' State, now replace the poet-as-ploughman (the obscure Neaira may suggest, *inter alia*, the new era). The cosmos becomes chaotic, and the poet seems trapped. The 'knucklebones' and 'hollow' golden ball – in part the once 'solid, homogeneous golden sphere' of true values mentioned in Mandelstam's 'Remarks on Chénier' – are the first of many devalued objects divested of function and meaning. The 'horse in the dust' evokes both Tsarist Russia and Pindar's Greece, amid the dimming memory of creative competition. The past, if rediscovered, is misappropriated (the horseshoe); if the poet's work survives, it will be disembodied, denatured, fossilized: stone, not bread. Thus the poet feels himself a counterfeit coin, having overestimated his own worth. He has lost the 'consciousness of being right' he once felt essential for poetry ('The Morning of Acmeism'). The logical consequence is silence.

SLATE ODE: This most complex poem primarily traces the poet's creative process from dark unconscious promptings to inspirational, revelatory clarity and a testing and acceptance of the Russian poets' 'flint path' of martyrdom. The essential subtexts are Derzhavin's despairing, unfinished last poem ('The river of times in its headlong course/Bears away all deeds of men ... ': a nihilistic assertion of impermanence which the poem's preservation paradoxically belies); Lermontov's evocation of the poet's solitary journey through life, beginning: 'I come out alone onto the road/The flinty path shines through the mist/The night is quiet. The wilderness hears God/And star speaks with star'; and Tyutchev's mythopoetic universe, of night and day, chaos and cosmos. Derzhavin's poem brings associations with the slate on which it was drafted, the lead pencil and perhaps the chalk with which Derzhavin wrote, and a famous portrait of the ageing poet, in a fur hat, beneath a high cliff in a mountain ravine washed by a stream.

The poem opens in awed representation of poetry's cosmic prove-nance and essence, the 'hardened' products of the juncture of time and inspirational fire, contrasting the subliminal and collective, intui-tive inarticulacy and even amnesia at the outset of the creative process. The 'terror' of stanza 2 is not political: it is the poet's 'holy terror' at the power of inspiration; the 'shifts' suggest the 'geological' shifts of the times as well as Mandelstam's leaps of auditory-semantic asso-ciation. Stanza 3 deals with poetry's audience and the social effect of its moral rectitude: the 'transparent forest ... ' may be the voices of poetic predecessors. The day of stanza 4 is presumably that of history, as a more personal, nocturnal, burning, honeyed, verbal rather than visionary inspiration takes shape. Maturing poetry is mixed with anger ('grapes of wrath'); knucklebones point to death, of youth or perhaps of the Tsar; but if stanza 5 deals also with the 'seamy side' of menace consequent upon creativity, in stanza 6 the emotionally charged creative voice takes authoritative, instantaneous shape. This is linked with the heightened self-awareness of a poet now in tune with creative night and historical day, confidently separate from the workers' state. His 'Beatitudes' suggest culture's martyr and redeemer, a conscious, morally discerning bearer of historical burden and cultural memory. As Jennifer Baines summarizes: 'The poet must plunge along the path of his forbears, to learn from them – the images of authority reappear in their previous form. Only by revering the past and allowing it to instruct him can he call himself the worthy inheritor of its great poetry. Only thus can he hope to equal its achievements.'

PARIS: Connected with Mandelstam's translations from Auguste Barbier's *Iambes*, vitriolic poems on what Mandelstam termed the 'classically unsuccessful revolution' of July 1830, 'born from a sense of contrast between the grandeur of the passing hurricane and the squalor of its results'. In an essay on Barbier with obvious relevance to himself and events in Russia, Mandelstam commended his 'revolutionary classicism' and ability to capture the essence of historical phenomena in single lines, despite not being an eyewitness to the events described. The poem combines familiar Mandelstamian motifs (horses, birds, trees and their felling, song, etc.) with images from Barbier: line 4, e.g., is from the latter's 'Le Lion' – where the lion is an image of popular revolt; the 'Phrygian grandmum' refers to the Revolution of 1789, and to the caps worn by liberated slaves in Ancient Greece; the baskets obviously evoke the guillotine; the months were renamed by decree of the Revolutionary Committee in 1793.

THE SKY IS PREGNANT WITH THE FUTURE: Written against the background of the Hague and Genoa Peace Conferences, the Rapallo Treaty between Germany and the USSR, and Mussolini's rise to power. Section 1 describes the emergence of the aeroplane, the key to power, observing a foreshortened enemy from the sky. Sections 2 and 3 seem to deal principally with anticipation of a Golden Age of peace, a higher phase of evolution, where poetry (wheat, honey-bees) can flourish in an organized, cosmic concord with distinctly Khlebnikovian overtones. There is reference to the destruction of German aviation under the Treaty of Versailles; the term for food in the third verse paragraph, *brashna*, suggests a meatless feast, in which (via Tyutchev) the chaos of night is covered over by the damask cloth. Section 4 begins despairingly: 'timelessness' (via Blok) is the present, anti-historical age, in which destructive pilots lack the conscience of beasts and war oppresses aspiring humanity. The conclusion seems deeply ambivalent: the pregnant sky may still promise harmony – or prove grotesquely indifferent and frighteningly unpredictable.

'LIKE A TINY LITTLE BODY WITH ITS WING': Another aeroplane-insect poem, a 'splinter in the azure' being an image for the 'living, animal charm of an aeroplane' in 'Cold Summer'. Here it also becomes an analogue for the poet (cf. the mosquito of 'I cannot know'). The primitive-primeval entity longs for a name – again, presumably, in order to enter the course of historical memory, and so be preserved into the future. There may also be an anti-militaristic theme of renunciation of destruction (further hints of a Golden Age).

1 JANUARY 1924: Begun in Kiev over Christmas, but the imagery suggests that it must have been completed in Moscow after Lenin's death

on January 21. To numerous echoes of Russian poetry, the plot shows the 'sick son' journeying in anguished solitude past the taverns and bureaucratic typewriters of night-time Moscow, in search of a magic cure.

Stanza 1 opens elegiacally. 'He' is the poet, who has shown the truth against the 'noise' of historical disintegration; the Russian for 'eyeball' also means 'apple' and 'orb', prompting associations of statehood; the twin eyeballs conceivably connote spiritual and temporal power.

Stanza 2: The poet ossifies alongside his 'cruel' and 'beautiful' age (cf. comparable oxymoronic combinations elsewhere); the state will soon compel him to silence through judicial execution.

Stanza 3: The 'understanding' poet is reluctant to stir himself, to recollect and create (the grasses) to cure future generations, not his own.

Stanza 4: He seeks escape – in space, since there is no escape in time – but the snow-covered road is a reproachful conscience-call to duty, the time-honoured self-immolatory role of the Russian intelligentsia.

Stanza 5: The compromise, a short, inconspicuous journey, is conducted in menacing disarray, yet with the re-emergence of genuine poetry (e.g. the frosty, apple-like crunch).

Stanza 6: Moscow's ironmongery in the hungry post-revolutionary winter presages the typewriter (the 'iron music of the age'). Moscow is 'again' the capital, with its ancient tradition of harsh injustice. The pike has ominous Russian folk and fable-connections.

Stanza 7: The chemist anticipates cure; the 'clicking' of bureaucratic orthodoxy mingles with horse's hooves of poetry, apprehension with self-delusion and asceticism as the escape gathers pace.

Stanza 8: Memories of childhood and sickness (peeling skin) suggest degradation into trivial, comfortable 'Sovietism'. 1920 was a terrible but, for Mandelstam, poetically triumphant year. The 'Fourth Estate' is the proletariat, but also the *déclassé* radical intellectuals of the nineteenth century; the Revolution did have purpose, which, as poetry (apple-snow) swells, the poet will not betray.

Stanza 9: The future remains ominous, despite the choice of allegiance: prescience of Terror and Mendacity brings no moral comfort. Behind the judgmental typewriter-key of the state and its poets is a magical, protective, redemptive talisman; but, as Ronen puts it, the metamorphosis of key to bone seems incomplete, and the poem ends in characteristic ambivalence, with an image of 'powerful moral harmony inadequately rendered, sorely missed, and ardently looked for'.

'NO, NEVER WAS I ANYONE'S CONTEMPORARY': Written in response to vituperative criticism of '1 January 1924', which both attacked the poet as an outmoded relic, and accused him of sycophantic accommodation to the times. See also his essay 'Storm and Stress': 'Blok was a contemporary ... of his time. Khlebnikov does not know what a contemporary is. He is a citizen of the whole of history, of the entire system of language and poetry'. The poet lingers and dies with the age – which has failed to 'forge another' after 1917 – but in dissociating from his contemporary namesake (the false image constructed by the critics?), he simultaneously transcends the era to become, in Ronen's words, 'its confessor' (cf. the eucharistic imagery at the close) and future communicant. The death recorded in stanzas 4–5 is probably that of Napoleon in exile (with tacit analogy to the recent death of Russia's secular Messiah, Lenin, and subtextual allusion to a recently dead Russian poet, Gumilyov), though Byron, or Russia's 'Decembrist' rebels of 1825, might also be implied. 'Whiteness' is one of the many subtle links to the preceding poem.

'YOU, LOW HOUSES': An ironic reworking of Prince Vyazemsky's exuberantly Russophile poem, 'Shrovetide in Foreign Parts' (1853), evidently connected with Mandelstam's move from Moscow in 1924. There are numerous hints at poetic resurgence: the potter's wares, the boots, the packet (lit. 'small sack') containing the ground coffee all belong, perhaps like St Petersburg itself, to Mandelstam's creative motifs. But the pike ribs of injustice and the dormant blades of the skates are signs of menace, just as Petersburg winters were not mild, and Petersburg itself, renamed Leningrad in January 1924, no longer existed. The tram (a reminiscence of the executed Gumilyov's 'Lost Tram'?) offers the 'last' lingering 'warmth' before cold silence.

'THIS NIGHT, IN ALL HONESTY': The real and the visionary intertwine in this creative nightmare, which draws on Pushkin's *Evgenii Onegin* and the deranged imaginings of Dostoevsky's Ivan Karamazov, but above all, of course, redeploys recurrent verbal motifs of Mandelstam's own cycle, and perhaps of his earlier *Tristia*. 'You can never get back the past' is something of a composite Pushkinian quotation: but to redeem the past is precisely the task of successful poetic creation.

'LIFE FELL LIKE A COUP DE FOUDRE': Addressed to Ol'ga Vaksel (1903–32), Mandelstam's passionate involvement with whom in winter 1924–5 almost lead to divorce (cf. line 3). The angel is from the façade of St Isaac's Cathedral, visible from the then Hotel Angleterre, where

Mandelstam and Vaksel used to meet. Abandoned by her husband, she lived with her two-year-old son (stanza 5) near the Tauride Palace and Gardens (stanza 7). At the time, Mandelstam felt that the poem betokened a new creative idiom.

'I WILL RUSH THROUGH THE GYPSY CAMP': A second poem to Vaksel – represented as 'cherry laurel branch' in snow-covered hood. The 'milling sound' is of Schubert's song-cycle *Die schöne Müllerin*, which Vaksel performed; his 'eternal' music recurs in two 1935 poems on Vaksel's death. The sleigh-runners may suggest handwriting; the frozen keys, of typewriter or piano, may also be the wooden pavements of Petersburg streets. The woman's presence is compellingly 'poetic'; but she is perhaps sought in vain. Echoes of Khlebnikov's war poetry are part of an undertone of panic, disorientation and growing isolation; and the sleigh-rug, made of bast, connoted the artist's death in an earlier poem by Mandelstam.

Boris Poplavsky

(24 May 1903–9 October 1935)

Translated by Belinda Cooke and by Richard McKane

BORIS POPLAVSKY, born in Moscow on May 24th 1903, belongs to the younger generation of the first emigration of Russian poets. After the 1917 Revolution he moved with his father to Yalta, where he was to experience some of the horrors of the Civil War and where his literary career was to begin. In 1919 they both emigrated to Constantinople and Poplavsky finally settled in Paris in 1921 where, apart from brief stays in Berlin, he was to live the rest of his short life until his tragic accidental death in October 1935. During his life, though he only published one book of poems (*Flags*, 1931) he commanded great respect both among his own peers as well as many of the older generation. Descriptions of Poplavsky's tragic end may have been glossed over by those wishing to preserve his memory but the story goes that he ran into a fellow drug addict intent on suicide, who somehow involved the poet. He died from an overdose of narcotics which may also have had some poison mixed in. Poplavsky was first introduced to drugs at the age of twelve by his sister (a cocaine addict), and regularly used hard drugs throughout his life, so there was always the risk that he might die in such circumstances. Volumes of his poetry published posthumously were: *Snowy Hour* (1936), *From a Garland of Wax* (1938) and *Airship of an Unknown Direction* (1965). He also completed one novel, *Apollo Unformed*, and started another, *Home from the Heavens*, as well as writing extensive journals.

Essentially Poplavsky's tragedy was that he was born at the wrong time. It was hard for the younger poets to gain access to the émigré journals controlled by the older established poets. Akhmatova, in 'Poem without a Hero' describes the plight of the Russian émigré: 'the air of exile is bitter like poisoned wine' but for those of Poplavsky's generation it was doubly bitter: they were deprived of any complete sense of the mother culture and excluded from established writer status which they might have achieved more readily had they stayed in Russia. In the poem 'Departure from Yalta', Poplavsky does express a sense of loss at leaving Russia; 'that we might believe, weep and burn with longing, / but never speak of happiness' but the more natural context for his poetry is the impoverished, bohemian setting of Paris where the poet is forced to make a living other than through his writing. Gleb Struve makes the scathing comment that Poplavsky 'did not know how to work and did not want to work', and though it is certainly true that Poplavsky never held down a paying job for more that a few days at a time, as a writer, considering his short life, he was extremely productive. Poets of Poplavsky's generation were also more ready to absorb the new culture and it is quite possible that he would have become a poet of the French language, indeed the influence of French poetry is very much present in his work.

The novel, and at times absurd, images which appear in Poplavsky's poetry are a reflection of his affinities with avant-garde movements such as French Surrealism and the Russian OBERIU. However, ultimately it is the poignancy of the poetry which gives it a lasting quality. His poetry is very personal with Poplavsky a Hamlet-like figure expressing the unbearable pain of living in the world. To reinforce this state of mind he frequently transfers this emotional state onto the natural world itself, 'the life of the woods grows sad on the mountains' and 'where with terrible voices the leaves on the trees / cry out in lament at their terrible destruction'. At the same time a line such as 'how endlessly touching is the evening' suggests that he is infinitely moved by this natural world, in spite of its bleakness. This ambivalence seems to be part of a search for something transcendent, mixed with fear that perhaps there is nothing else, expressed either with moving directness, 'Everything now is meaningless and clear / be at peace there is nothing more', or on the edge of despair, 'It's terrible to think how time passes / you can neither think nor live'. One is left feeling though, not that Poplavsky had a death wish but more that he is absorbed in a kind of pleasurable melancholy, indeed that such a glorification of melancholy is what provides him with a purpose. This said, Poplavsky in his poetry and life interested himself in a wide range of beliefs. He is however predominantly focused on a traditional Christian God, although his relationship with this God is expressed rather oddly as a close friendship between two ordinary people, 'I don't believe in God myself / but I see how fragile we both are' and 'God called to me but I didn't reply, we felt shy and cursed our shyness'.

As far as translation of Poplavsky's poetry is concerned his wordplay loses a lot in translation, yet at other times his poems are a gift for the translator: the novel ways in which he personifies nature, the 'heartbreaking' quality of many of his direct statements, and the beautiful sense of movement in some of his images, all can be conveyed into English without great loss; by way of example of this last quality consider these lines from 'Salome':

> ... to the song
> of the white acacia, the evening walked away ...
> beyond the river and into the clouds.

> ... The restaurant
> orchestra swam over the marsh
> and into the interminable distance.

Nikolay Tatischev, who was instrumental in publishing much of Poplavsky's poetry after his death, tells us: 'Poplavsky loved those overcast Parisian winters and to watch the poor and the wealthy and their states of mind'. Many of the poems in this selection show Poplavsky as this outsider expressing affinities with the various isolated street figures who walk through his poems. We see here how Poplavsky managed to find in an alien landscape, a context for powerful poetry – the poetry of the Russian poet exiled in more ways than one.

Useful texts in reference to Poplavsky's life and work:

Berberova, Nina: *The Italics are Mine*. Chatto & Windus, 1991

Carlisle, Olga: *Poets on Street Corners: Portraits of Fifteen Russians*. New York: Random House, 1968

Karlinsky, Simon and Alfred Appel, Jr.: *The Bitter Air of Exile: Russian Writers in the West 1922–1972*. Berkeley: University of California Press, 1977

Poplavsky, Boris: *Collected Works of Boris Poplavsky*. 3 volumes (in Russian) Berkeley: University of California Press, 1980

Poplavsky, Boris: *Stikhotvoreniya*. Tomsk: Vodoley, 1997

Poplavsky, Boris: *Sochinenya*. St Petersburg: Letny Sad, 1999

Poplavsky, Boris: *Sochinenya*. 3 volumes. Moscow: Soglasie, 2000

Belinda Cooke

Pity for Europe

To Marc Slonim

Europe. Europe. With what slow, youthful mourning
your immense flags are stirring in the moonlit air.
Amputees speak laughingly of war
while the scientist in the park prepares a rocket to the moon.

Bright flags are raised on the tall buildings.
The clock dreams on the tower. Will the experiment be a success?
The sun sinks into the sea with the slow decline
of summer days. The ship disappears in a strip of smoke.

But the soft autumn rain flies onto the lilac road.
The cinema resounds and the teenager buys a ticket.
And in a sky heavy with rain, the mysterious, winged genius
dreams, high up in his skyscraper, of future happiness.

Europe. Europe. Your gardens are full of people.
Ophelia reads a newspaper in a white taxi
while Hamlet is dreaming of departing to freedom on a tram,
fallen under the wheels with a smile of deathly longing.

The immense sun is setting in the yellow mist.
Far, far off in the suburbs gaslights burst into flame.
Europe. Europe. The boat is sinking in the ocean,
as the orchestra in the hall blasts out a prayer on trumpets.

Everyone remembered the trams, the woods and autumn.
Everyone plunged deep in sadness in this pale blue abyss.
Tell me – Are you afraid? Am I afraid? Not really!
I'm a European! laughed the man in evening dress.

I'm English you see. I'm used to the ice in newspapers.
I'm used to submitting, to losing with dignity. And yet,
in London such delicate ladies approach their 'friends',
while shop roses are withering behind thick glass.

The genius on the tower was dreaming of the future:
in his vision blue glass buildings in the distance,
where angels borne on wings of freedom
flew from the cold earth to the sun to grieve.

And once more sunsets shone over the roofs of the towers
where, in love with the sky, they sang of eternal spring.
The following morning people wept from a terrible pity,
having seen the past years by chance in a dream.

Empty boulevards. The soft rain has fallen and become
      weary,
huddled up against the fence in the cold autumn languor.
There where we died expecting nothing for ourselves –
we, the sick workers of the too tall house: –

under the white stones in the cold yellow dawn,
peaceful as the years, as the drowning duke in evening dress,
like the old professor singing quietly in the dark,
flying off in his iron rocket to the murderous stars.

1930   [BC]

Stoicism

In that warm hour over the darkened world
the yellow-nosed moon was born,
to be immediately wiped clean with soap:
and at once sensed autumn and the garden.

All day heat had resounded from the tower,
while the people's eyes saw a dream before death . . .
It is late before evening, the sorcerer
smiled, refreshing with his dark crimson robes.

Under the green twilight of the chestnut trees
the darkish lilac granite was drying out.
The children laughed loudly by the fountain,
drawing the new town with chalk.

In the morning birds were washing themselves
in the aqueduct, while the emperor slept on bare boards.
Already, among the marble and boredom,
a midday hell was breathing from the Euphrates.

But over the castle, beneath a deathly sky,
the immense golden wings stretched out,
and a lifeless victory was smiling
as the soldier lay dozing beneath a layer of dust.

It was stifling. In the wretched bath house
things were stolen, as beggars were shaved;
while in the water we talked of realms,
with a cautious movement of lips.

We spoke of the fine way this world had been silenced,
of how it had been consumed, of how it was evening
in Rome. We spoke of the marvellous, wrongful
death of the broad-shouldered children of wise men.

Glistening athletes were jeering
as the yellow moon flamed up.
But Christ bowed down over Lethe
and listened to us in the awful distance.

The night stars were melting in the sea
and flowers were escaping from the heat.
Indian kings, already awoken, were making
their way over the abyss into Bethlehem.

And the servant of sleeping Pilate
quietly poured water into the bowl,
while the centurion on duty cleaned the armour
and Joseph sullenly planed the cross.

1930   [BC]

Winter

To Abram Minchin

The pink light sinks to the white valley.
The sun rises to study the sky of the soul.
An angel dances in the rays with a golden mandolin.
Reeds are glittering in the park of frozen trees.

Winter morning sets in with the glimmer of snow.
Eternity falls silently on your warm arm.
Pure eternity falls to the body like tenderness,
and disappears pressing onto the incarnate spirit.

The dead sun dozes on the pink iceberg.
The prison orchestra plays quietly in the dungeon.
The black souls went down beneath the earth with torches
while into the sky rose the sacred shadows of those in love.

The snow of the universe falls in the black air.
The maid of the dawn wanders among the carriages.
Behind her, silently, with a sorrowful inclining of their heads,
the drowsy, yellow spectres of gaslights march along.

Everything falls asleep. On the towers the giants are silent.
Everything is transformed towards the strange morning hours.
Like a big, whitish cockroach going into a black heart,
the grey sky crawls towards the naked corpses.

1930   [BC]

The Flags are Lowered

Over the rows of grey sarcophagi
where the blind street lamp was already burning,
soaked by rain, the angel of flags
continued to incline over the crowd.

The street is lit up with the glow of street lamps,
but higher up the early dark mixes with chimney smoke.
The man under the slender black roof
walks slowly in the darkness towards morning.

Fine, transparent sheets of rain
flood across the lights of the tram.
Through the shop window the wax maiden
looks out wildly at the unearthly cold.

All is gloomy, peaceful and brutal.
High in the sky in your bright vestments
you shone. Now you must come down
from your flagstaff and return to ordinary life.

Sleep. Forget. Everything was so fine.
But very, very soon, over Your lodging
the new angel in red, white and blue
will happily take wing in the azure sky.

Because the eternal holiday drags on
the birds are hiding, the chimneys fly off.
Time is extinguished. Again we dream of morning
and wax muses on the fires of hell.

The sun comes in like a golden standard.
Thoughts perish. The sky turns pink.
The evening fades. The sun rushes into the morning
and night does not dare conceal the dawn.

Alright then, fall. You used to light up the prison.
You used to shine, accepting the terror of the skies.
Asleep, or awake, we only dream of love.
You, like happiness, are needed by no one.

1931   [BC]

'Hamlet's shadow'

Hamlet's shadow, a passer-by without a coat.
Crows are sleeping in the pale blue gardens.
But startled by the sound of a far-off whistle
ravens shake down cotton wool from the branches.

You go out for a walk. Your hand caresses the snow.
You go out onto the tram with the rest.
You fall asleep in a café. You find peace in wine.
You escape into the unreal world of the cinema.

But what sort of tramp is this – at this time of day?
It is Christ, of course, in the Salvation Army.
The day, in sickly decline, was now fading fast.
Everything was quiet on the Sunday night.

Along the immaculate whiteness the tracks
run back and forth crossing paths.
Where did he go—avoiding disaster? He
suddenly decided he was late and far from home.

Here are the tracks of hands. Here is a snowball.
Everyone has vanished. The wind sweeps up everything.
Everything is locked. The Lord's house is silent, while
the sick man, in luxury, is reading through the night.

Everything has become confused as the print
strains the eyes. How slowly the hours, whole
sections of time crawl by. The lift rises monotonously,
with its whining voice. How bored are the lonely ones.

Suddenly the clattering of a tram. No one notices.
Everything has been in a whirl, has disappeared, or melted.
The face of the people meets the snow with a smile –
how easy it is for them and how silent it has become.

But his Death sits opposite on the armchair
and gazes around at the walls with a smile.
Having known these poems for such a long time,
he simply reads the crumpled newspaper.

Death knows the heat will die down, and he will
forget everything. Suddenly – a blow from the darkness:
there is snow in the room and lips blue from cold.
what can I make of this – haven't you had enough of terror?

When the heat dies down and the day rises
it is time to part. In the morning the snow will melt,
the cheerful postman will come with a letter
and how quickly we shall forget this Sunday suffering.

Unable to live and suddenly unawares . . .
the lamp goes out, the windows fly open.
– Does this mean that I am exhausted?
– There is no time to think. Time forgets.

But the poor beggar must always contend
with the snow and the damp stone.
He hates the street lamps in the mist.
You see, my friend, he is not deceived by poetry.

He sings a song to the drum beat in a blue uniform.
Lord for pity's sake! You gave me the pain
of Your terrible wounds. I understand You well.
You are close to me. I love You dearly.

I eat Your bread. You drink my tea in the corner.
The flame sings out in the stove. With drowsy eyes
the ass and the ox on the stone floor
are reading a book as night draws to a close.

1931   [BC]

'How cold it is'

How cold it is. The empty soul is silent.
Over the town today the snow is born.
It quickly flew from the sky and melted.
Everything was quiet. The world stopped.

Turn on the lights. How quickly it has become dark.
The bright placards have disappeared from the houses.
It is night on the bridge, where, concealed in white smoke
soldiers got soaked as they played snowballs.

The earth glitters. Bare branches strain upwards.
The icy boulevards are glistening with mica.
In the secretive, deathly-still splendour,
the sky is darkening, heavy with water.

Beneath the snow and rain, we are reading our poems
to the embittered passers-by. Bear with it
my exhausted friend. Let's wait a little . . .
It's time for us to sleep. We can no longer wait.

How cold it is. The soul asks for mercy.
Be resigned, sleep – there is no mercy for the weak.
January is silent and each day carries away
the last heat of the soul, the last light.

Close your eyes and let someone else play.
Lie there in your coat. Wrap up warm and be quiet.
The crow croaks as it shakes snow onto the garden.
The wood-stove drones monotonously.

Drink up your wine. Let's read our poems to one another.
Let's forget the world. For me the world is unbearable.
It is nothing but weakness, a sunny snowstorm
in the fatal glow of unearthly winters.

The lights burn. The pedestrians have disappeared.
The centuries fly by in the gloom of dumb imprisonments.
Everything is only a snowstorm of golden freedom,
dreamed of pain to the rays of dawn.

January 1932   [BC]

'At that hour when your eyes'

At that hour when your eyes are too tired to write,
and it's impossible to talk to anyone,
there in the garden above the black bushes
the Milky Way burns late in the night.

Enough. Enough. Nothing is necessary.
There is nothing to reproach happiness for.
Far better in the dark, over the black garden,
to be quiet thus, to hide and shine.

Down below, close to despair, people sleep
both from happiness and labour.
Only the beggar listens to the silence
and wanders off into nowhere.

He sits, solitary, on the bench in the park
and looks upwards, chained to the winter –
thinking, there are so many stars,
how brightly my terrible destiny burns.

Grief had been suddenly forgotten
for a moment ... But here again, it is
naked and brooding, and having cursed
your poem, you will slowly close the window.

1931   [BC]

'The sadness of fields'

I

The sadness of fields lies in the haze.
The golden sun is scarcely visible;
it plays in the heavy stained glass
where the sacred flame is glimmering.

It is silent in the cold church.
Everything has been washed clean by hand.
Only the lamp raised on the altar
glimmers through the ages.

The stone itself is alive with holy water.
Everything sleeps, but the dream of the church
is radiant ... the young priest
gently raises the chalice at dawn.

Gracefully, deliberately he intones
the familiar age-old words,
while dawn is still in flames –
an unearthly light beyond the clouds.

And the bell in the misty hour
slowly sends out its voice.
It does not wake us from mortal dreams.
It does not judge, only offers a blessing.

2

The sun shines gently in the mist.
The smoke rises like an immovable pillar.
Already a carriage clatters between the houses.
Life is waking up in the blue.

The light hoarfrost has melted on the roofs.
The language of the bells has fallen silent.
Everything is white as before– except high up
where patches of blue appear and disappear.

Today I woke so early.
I slept so long, but I cannot remember my dreams.
I smiled at the whitish-grey day.
I was ready to forgive and forget guilt.

But my mood blackened in anticipation,
my thoughts darkened, became plunged in blackness.
I went out to people – and couldn't face it.
I searched my soul – there was doubt and terror.

But then out of the icy rain
I walked into this empty church
where the lamp hovers over the earth,
not troubled by my anger or grief.

Thinking did not resolve the pain
but only darkened it further.
Suddenly tears burst out, my heart opened.
My calmness returned.

The new cathedral was silently flooded with light.
The tranquil priest came in.
I heard the organ and forgot myself.
I renounced both anger and grief.

3

In the cold yellowish sky
over the gutters where water is rushing
in the winter sky smoke rises from the towns
incessantly like the craving for bread.

The cumbersome train rattles the bridges.
A sign appears: 'Tabac'.
Gaslights catch fire and then go out.
The pub doors are opening.

The conductor crawled in and the guard blew the whistle.
The train carriages shunted along in the snow.
And from early morning I have lost touch with life.
I have to keep going, but I can no longer go on.

The first snow reminded me of the past,
of fate, the earth, You.
I dressed and left the rooms.
I calmed my sorrow in walking.

But the noise glides in vain
by the white palaces like a river within its shores.
It's the same pain on the roads.
It's the same grief in the snows.

No, you don't need support in the dark;
you've got what you need – height and purity,
the freedom of high mountains,
the snow-covered roofs of the small monastery.

For a long time the storm will make roads impassable.
Then night will pass and the snow will calm down.
Quietly the wicket gate will knock, and the passer-by
will find the long-awaited lodging.

The light of the lamp is soft and simple
it signifies peace. Lie down.
Tomorrow you will rise like the snowy morning
and calmly you will get stuck into life.

But for you on the street, where is your monastery?
At home I bow down closely to my work.
But for you convict, where is your home?
Where the church bells ring – it's there.

1931   [BC & RM]

'The grass is born'

The grass is born. The road breathes with heat.
The islands feast their eyes on the river.
The soul is silent. It doesn't listen to itself.
The soul lives in everything. The soul is dead.

Spring rises. The soul is weary.
It is silent and empty from constant suffering.
The sickness I feel is the sickness
of the world from the first days of sin.

Under the white sun the grass comes to life.
The world warms up and work is far away.
Peacefully across the river, Your hand
reaches towards the white clouds.

You speak without understanding yourself,
too far away from the words
and the mute river suddenly awakes into words
and the clouds transform into words.

On the bronze road over the water
we speak, born in hell.
Saved once again by destruction and fate,
we weigh in the sky the ashes of souls.

The river gets lost beyond the islands.
The bathhouse is thrilled with the sunny spot.
The Sibyl hides herself behind the words.
Life repeats itself speaking of nothing special.

Calmly, distracted and motionless, You gaze at the stones
of the bridge, then screw up your eyes at the light.
The cloud passes in the distance blotting out our lives
and again happiness eludes us.

1930   [BC]

'Over the sunny music of the water'

Over the sunny music of the water
where the shore tore itself from the cliff into the sea,
the forests blossom and the white smoke
of spring clouds dissolves in the morning patrol.

Again I rose with my soul from the winter's dark
and here in the mountains behind the grey agave
the world opened out for me once more
with its tormenting and sun-filled amusement.

Resin flows in silence to the orange earth.
The scarcely audible distant noise
reminds me that the sea heeds
unhurriedly as it covers the edge of the earth.

Spring is silent. All is clear to me without a word:
how painful for me, yet how easy to breathe.
I'm here once more. It's painful for me again in the world.
I am not able to interfere with anything.

The surf rustles on the telegraph network
and the foam beats, hurrying into the street
and the primeval wind is miraculously young:
its soul remembers nothing.

The sky was covered with dark blue,
swirling it found a white cloud in the sun
and surrounding itself with a fiery strip
it slid off to the glass of the heavens.

In an inexplicable gold movement,
granting to fate with a miraculous humility,
not seeing myself in the light reflection,
in disparagement, not crying about myself

I lie in the hot heather, forgetting
how long I've been suffering and living.
I close my eyes, hot in the sun
and again I love You forever.

1934   [RM]

'Today my heart is full to the brim'

Today my heart is full to the brim
with the modulated sound of carefree waves,
before you I am again the shining seabed
of earthly fate, eternally playing.

All the life of the soul is in the eyes, of nature in the sea
and every dawn another beauty
is born in it, not knowing grief
and in the evening it is more beautiful than by day.

I have known from my youth the depth
of high-flown suffering, but not having found peace
now I believe and listen to the wave singing
that happiness is deeper than peace.

The undarkened day filled the forest
with its warmth and got lost in its heart.
The low house is full of restful happiness
illuminated by the shining cloud.

Here where the soul lives in happy wildness
looking at the peaceful world through the conifer forest,
in October Sagittarius has not yet sent
his arrow into the autumn silence.

Far off the mountain forest is turning yellow
where the swallows have rushed with brief screams,
the soul is silent, subdued by the tiredness
of the earth, heeding the power of autumn.

Tired of paying attention to the midday moisture
it thinks about an underground dream,
about again living in the ravine
where the elderberry has clothed itself in berries.

Under another name, but with the same exhilaration
like the shining fate of airy transformations
the swifts, rushing away, sing about
what's going on in the field's border.

The same light burns in all worlds,
all the centuries sound out one refrain
and I too am immortal in them as the day in the mountains
is immortal and always seems like the first one.

Recognize yourself in the warmth of the evening.
Sacred happiness everywhere gives birth to life.
It is in you, it is around, everywhere.
It always accompanies love.

1933   [RM]

'The summer evening is heavy and dark'

To V. Varshavsky

The summer evening is heavy and dark,
the stifling wind rustles like paper,
a yellow aura surrounds
the disc of the moon, rising over the ravine.

A bright light rose and perished
over the crests of the gigantic lime trees.
All around was concussed by the black thunder.
The rain drummed on the house.

The dusty bushes, jammed among the barns,
rocked in the yard
and the streams sparkled out of the darkness,
calling like a crane among the porch piles.

The birds have been chased from night rest in the thicket,
the water-dust flies at the house windows
but the brighter the rain rushes from the sky
the quicker its hubbub stills.

The black forest falls silent, yet still rustling
with damp firs beyond the column of the swing
and the garden breathes in a glimmering drop
with the aching smell of pines.

Opening the tall dacha's window,
departing for a moment from words and thoughts
the failure listened motionlessly
to the happy diminuendo.

He thought that the world was younger
than the politically correct city dandies
but his soul cannot accept
the dark and arrogant people's tears;

that the earth and happiness are deeper than pain
because death is necessary for the forests
so that grass in spring could burst into freedom,
rain to earth, birds to sky;

that sadness without belief is darker than a lie
and sick pity more bitter than anger.
Slowly in the calm, grey smoke
the day, that the oriole was calling, rose.

The first ray, miraculously bright
passed over the crests of the washed pines
and the long, calm, hot day
began with the fussing of birds in the bushes.

1932–3   [RM]

Home from the Heavens

To N. Postnikova

The fate of the soul cannot be disclosed by words.
Again we're deprived here of freedom in the rays of rain,
the spring wind breathes to the islands
and mud sparkles in the field in the weak sun.

The earth in the forest, having heard the weak splash,
fluttered its eyelashes of rain,
it slept among the pine stars
as though it had forgotten to breathe and live.

In the leaden sky the still empty
crimson canopy soars over the meadow.
How quietly, listen my dear, the brown
ice-blocks thaw on the bank.

Look how like my love
is the empty tenderness of the unworked field.
It has woken again in the rays of rain
but not begun to live as it remembers something.

The dried-up fields are in the dust of rays.
The earth has suffered under the bright sky
in the golden confinement of last summer,
waited for rain, cracked with pain.

The sunset shone in dust in the smoke of the thunderstorm
and the colour of pages changed from lightning,
but only the forest burnt by the autumn in the distance
waited long enough for the long-awaited peace.

The peace of spring, he who knows you
will never abandon this earth.
In the cold sky, in the joyful prayer
the swallows rush, recognizing the road.

Home from the heavens to the scarcely audible rustle of
      grasses
from afar to the landslips of hillsides.
They did not want to live so close to the sun,
they fly, they will return soon.

In the leaden sky like the ghost of spring
the crimson canopy of birches is motionless.
In vain does one see dreams in the dark of graves –
you can't guess at the peace of vernal life.

How unnoticeably did joy blossom.
Here is the low house and we are by the target.
The spring rain rustled in the shade of the trunk.
We listened for a long time and didn't dare talk.

1934   [RM]

'Cold, ruddy from sleep'

Cold, ruddy from sleep,
the face of dawn leaned over the earth.
You're here again, spring, my spring,
alone with me in the silence of daybreak.

A scarcely heard hubbub arose in the empty forest,
there a dead leaf warms the living earth
and a sombre spring reflects
the light of a cloud soaring over the birch tree.

The dew of the heights in the mossy gully
sparkles with crystal eyelashes.
The heart waits, for long it has not slept,
to meet the bright light in the clean branches.

The water has calmed overnight
and you can hear in the distance the splash of a fish.
Circles widen and dissolve without trace.
Life is closer, the sky sparkles brighter.

The spring forest suddenly flared all in sunlight,
warmed by the effulgent river.
It suddenly met the sun, as here
we met each other and peace.

I look at the world, where new centuries,
oblivious of heaven, enter life.
Spring the beauty has come from afar
and the empty world motionlessly observes.

The heavens still do not melt in the distance,
leaden over the damp black earth,
the birds' voices cannot be heard in the ravine
and the dirty snow lies in the green forest.

Only weak thunder, scarce heard, casts spells
in the shining of clouds full of heavy moisture.
Soul, it seems you have got ready to live
and you look and try to remember your homeland.

Under grave eyelashes eyes
are striving to the limit of known pain
where in the distance the storm is doomed
to sparkle and noisily pour out on the field.

All more joyfully, more strongly loving the world,
laughing and breaking the bonds of sorrow
I live here, I met You here,
I call You the rain sound.

1934   [RM]

Daniel Andreyev

(2 November 1906–30 March 1959)

Translated by Richard McKane and Vladimir Baskayev,
Richard McKane and Belinda Cooke

DANIEL ANDREYEV was born in Berlin, the son of the outstanding Russian novelist and short story writer Leonid Andreyev. His mother died shortly after his birth and his aunt, Elizaveta Dobrova, took him into her family in Moscow. The family and city were to become his own throughout his happy childhood. He started writing poems and prose as a child, a huge epic where the action revolved round interplanetary space. In his youth he experienced metaphysically the dark and dangerous side of life and without these insights he would not have written much of what he wrote.

Daniel Andreyev loved nature deeply and was in constant wonder at the spirit of creation. He could be called a 'green' poet before his time. In the country he walked barefoot whenever he could, usually alone, with sparse supplies of food (he ate very little) and tobacco.

He met his wife-to-be, an artist, Alla Bruzhes, in 1937 while he was still living with the Dobrovs. Before the war Daniel Andreyev worked on a novel, *Strangers of the Night*, which he buried in the ground before he was mobilized as a non-combatant private (because of his health) at an HQ outside Moscow and then with an infantry division on convoy duty across the icebound Ladoga Lake for Leningrad under siege. His long poem 'Leningrad Apocalypse' in 133 octets describes this. He spent the last months of the war, which had seriously traumatized him, as a graphic artist (a trade he had learnt before the war).

When he dug up his novel the ink he had written it in had run. He rewrote it this time on a typewriter which his father had left in Moscow. He collaborated on a book on Russian travellers in Africa (including Nikolay Gumilyov, his favourite poet). The secret police came for him on 21 April 1947, with the excuse that he was to be taken to Kharkov to give a lecture on the Africa book. Two days later they searched the house and found the manuscript of the novel. The investigation of the Andreyevs lasted nineteen months – thirteen in the Lubyanka and six in Lefortovo Prison, and sucked in many friends who had heard or read parts of the novel and his poems. The interrogation was even based on the heroes of the novel as though they were living people. The prosecution's case was broadened to include a plot against Stalin, yet the Andreyevs were not political. Since the death sentence had been abolished recently, Daniel Andreyev was sentenced to twenty-five years in prison and Alla Andreyeva to twenty-five years hard labour in camp.

It was in Vladimir Prison, one hundred miles from Moscow, that Daniel Andreyev embarked on the three interconnected books for which he is justly famous in Russia: *Russian Gods* (a book of cycles of poetry), *The Rose of the World,* a many-layered, philosophical, cosmological, and metaphysical work (which has been compared to such different works as Dante's *The Divine Comedy* and Tolkien's *The Lord of the Rings*) which is now translated into English and published by Lindisfarne, and *The Iron Mystery* (a play in verse). Though the prison cell was liable to random searches he managed, with the cooperation of his cellmates, some of whom were common criminals, to conceal the scraps of paper on which he had written. But the real miracle of the survival of his work was when he was finally released from Vladimir Prison after the Khrushchev Review Commission on Political Prisoners in 1956: the Governor of the prison (a certain Krot whose name means 'mole') gave over to Alla Andreyeva a whole sack of his writings and personal effects that he had decided to leave in Vladimir Prison when he was transferred to the Lubyanka for the rest of his term that had been reduced to ten years.

Much of Daniel Andreyev's writing was written at night and is visionary. He had already had a heart attack while he was in prison and the couple of years that he had left to live after he was released in April 1957, in poor health, he devoted to rewriting, editing and finishing the three books mentioned above, which he must have known might never be published in Russia.

His widow, Alla Andreyeva, is the preserver of his heritage. I met her in Moscow in 1989, through my friend Arkady Rovner who had given me a typescript of *The Rose of the World* in 1979, when I was on a Fellowship at Princeton. At that time I did not know that Daniel Andreyev's poems existed, but the book convinced me that Daniel Andreyev was a true poet. *Russian Gods*, which includes poems, poems in prose and 'symphonies of poems' from the 1930s to the 1950s, is designed in cycles as a 'poetic ensemble', as he called it. He wrote most of this book in Vladimir Prison, taking the images of his lucid dreams, experiencing mystical revelations and insights. He believed that all nature, creatures, rivers, trees and lakes are living souls. He was also of the generation that lived under the threat of nuclear war and tyranny. His life and art dwell constantly on the struggle of light and darkness, good and evil, but his belief in the forces of light helped him to survive as a human being in what was arguably the most terrifying time in the history of Russia.

In the early 1990s in Russia, Daniel Andreyev became known as an outstanding visionary and philosopher. His book *The Rose of the World* was published in Moscow in print runs totalling almost a million and a four-volume edition of his works came out (Moskovsky Rabochy and Urania). Finally Alla Andreyeva brought out her book of memoirs *Sailing to the Heavenly Kremlin* (Urania, Moscow 1998) which tells the story of the great and enduring love of this remarkable couple as well as being a chronicle of those harsh times.

The unchronological order of the poems is a result of the poems being taken from his poem-cycles in Volumes 1 and 3 in the Moskovsky Rabochy and Urania Edition, edited by Alla Andreyeva and B.N. Romanov.

These translations are published with permission of the Urania Foundation, dedicated to the work of Daniel Andreyev.

Richard McKane
London, May 2000

Pushkin's Monument

Thick-lipped boy, garrulous rake,
how was he able to overpower himself?
Having tasted the living Parnassian wine from the Muse's cup,
how did he pour the spirit and flesh into the harmony of Russia?

The iron enmity of warring camps,
of discordant truths, of storming ideas
is humbled here, facing Titans
like this Tsar, child and sorcerer.

Here, raised high in bronze over the storms, the battle, the blood,
he silently listens to the centuries' hymn of praise
in which roar, the prayers of mystics and the Bolsheviks' march
are fused with the glorification of the empire.

He sees tears of rapture from a height,
he senses the warm current of love triumphant . . .
Master of beauty! Confidant of the Eternal Rose!
Bless! Declare! Donate! Father sons!

It seems that the granite pedestal, warmed by
the people's hands, by the warmth of numberless lips,
is our symbol, our covenant, the sacred stone of Moscow,
the magic crystal of love and creation.

1950

Stanzas

Worlds swirl in a stormy haze
over every colossus city:
the hundred-voiced choirs are countless
and the currents of life are layer upon layer.

I catch their splashing chaos
at the clear, sober, loud midday,
not at night, in the crazy rotas of reveries,
not in torn dreams, not when tipsy.

Through the circle of elements, the souls of buildings,
through the hosts of those who once were people,
sense the eyes of monstrous creations
with a watchful gaze.

Be bold! The ancient demon is visible
before your eyes, through the breach:
he has moved the cone of darkness like a helmet
hiding his stormy face.

He is drunk with an alien power
and thirst, cutting as a knife –
with such torture, anger and passion
that you will turn back your look in anger.

Others hurry to fight with him:
their flight is striking and grand,
the sense of their actions is the liturgy
of forces and rights which we cannot understand.

The great spirit's crown touches the sky
and he is scarcely outlined in the future,
the creator of the people
with a sunny mansion in his breast.

Hovering outside the world of numbers and measures,
flooding the layers of the universes with light,
the *World Salvaterra* burns
a ray into us, like a new myth.

Where even the genius is powerless
in the hours of the prophetic dream,
the look is lost in the waterspouts of visions,
not able to touch the bottom.

1949

Christmas Eve

Dedicated to Alla Andreyeva

Speech fell silent in the doorway.
Everyone left. We're alone. The two of us.
We'll light up the living constellations
as in our blessèd childhood.

There is a smell of wax and the pine forest.
The tiled stove is white and hot.
Above the decorated Christmas tree
candle after candle lights up.

The dancing balls sway
in the warm current of air.
Over there, high on the branches,
the flowers and worlds of an eternal fairy tale.

The Radiant Mother is looking at
the adorned festive table
and its white tablecloth
and Her aura is twinkling.

These two most beautiful last candles
are for Her, the Bride of Heaven.
Let them shine all together,
holy and inseparable in their light.

Only together, yes, together
in their dying act and beyond . . .
The sign of God is in this News
for the two of us – forgotten and wretched.

1949

'The stars on the Kremlin towers'

The stars on the Kremlin towers do not sparkle.
The crowd does not surge by the platform.
Be vigilant! It's black in the moonless capital
as an ice-hole in winter.
Only the long searchlights cut
the distant, quartered sky,
casting their rays of light
deep into the starry depths.

The fires have long ago burnt out
in the wastelands of the German rear.
The ashes of Novgorod and Oryol
have long ago grown cold.
The night hammers at
the cast iron door of the horizon:
the enemy is here! The surrounding haze
trembles in the lightning at the front.

When the empty heights resound
with an ever-growing drone
and the crowds hurry

into the underground honeycombs
muttering about the end,
the parabolas of fantastic stars,
green, silver, crimson
sparkle like a miracle
on the dull night's purple.

Read! The huge millstone is grinding
the seeds of vengeance.
Constellations rush and die,
lightning howls over the roofs.
The living apocalypse of the century
is happening in the skies and in the dust.
Read! These ancient manuscripts are the landmarks
of peoples, countries and epochs.

December 1941

Without Honours

If it is fated to meet the end,
soon – now – here,
for what purpose is this surf
of ever growing powers?

And why, in strong-willed dreams
does the gold of thoughts boil
as if I am looking into the volcano's mouth,
blinded by the lava glitter.

Who, and why, like a Cyclops,
piles on me the rubble,
concepts for which the narrow
life of the poet is too short?

And as for those who did not complete
their life's vocation – here,
does death throw open the gates
for its fulfilment *there*?

1950

'An old wood-goblin'

An old wood-goblin, or a grey wolf:
they are all buried in the thickets and the wilds:
their conversations with people are over
and they cannot achieve new souls,
souls, which today held power,
so as to go away or fall tomorrow.

But Russia accepted me
into its dwelling within:
I sense her secret concepts,
the striving and the passion
and the star that ascended into the silence
of her unread soul.

Obedient to this star alone,
rich with this star alone,
I hear in the rustle of ferns in the pine forest,
in the wilful choruses of flocks of geese,
the germination of ancient seeds
and the universe's garden of the future.

In the stormy joy of bad weather,
in its illegal revelry
and in the radiant eyes of the people
and in their darkest fate,
in the young, who are happy to listen to,
even in the age of canals, the tale of Kitezh city.

And I study – through the roar of machines,
the talk, swearing and wingless laughter,
the rustle of women fussing like mice,
the hurried schedules, the uproar of fun –
I study so that I can listen to what the people
still aren't conscious of themselves.

I search for friends – not arrogant or vulgar ones,
but those who are rich in dreams –
not in committees, nor in clubs
nor in the warm comfort of huts
but in the twinkling of eyes meeting,
in the unspoken words of chance phrases.

1950

Ancient

Above the river, before the deserted evening
the nomad bonfire was crackling
and the mists, pale blue as superstitions,
rose from the overgrown lakes.

From behind the chalk promontory, along the bend,
passing the reflecting hill
I saw a boat approaching
with green branches in the rowlocks.

Rapid, smooth, mysterious
it was a shade of grey in the advancing darkness
and on its curved prow the Master himself
did not stir the single oar.

His beard was bluish-black and his hair
like a knightly, forest beauty:
he wore only a linen shirt without a belt
and home-made canvas trousers.

With such a look a woodsman and falconer
could take in at a glance the predatory taiga;*
with such power the two-fingered schism
was strengthened in the monasteries on the bank.

The forest deities surrendered
before this faith, before this flaming freedom
and he glides through the twilight, the powerful one,
the shepherd of the forest, its priest, its head.

That midnight, as I threw branches
into the wild flames, I prayed to the former darkness –
together with the thousand-faced forest spirits,
with the bitter and pure pitch.

1945–1950

* The coniferous forest belt of the subarctic northern continents.

'Oh, how glorious it is'

Oh, how glorious it is to take off one's shoes on a spring day!
Greetings my dear, cool earth,
the copses flooded with light and without shadow
and the meadows without grass and dock.

Prickly and grey, like the hands of a grubby child,
the stains of snow melt all around
and in the blackening gully it is recorded
how the children ran around here barefoot.

To lose oneself with no backward looks in the thicket,
in the quiet rustling of the greening crowd
and laughing heels softly tread
on the resilient, drying out path.

The earth is so brilliant,
all saturated with living joy,
moist and tender, icy, naked
with blueness splashing quietly in the puddles.

The nostrils breathe in the sweet-smelling road,
the roots, the humus, the grass
and you could let life slip by in your lair
if you had never felt this.

1931–1950

'The air, singing in the winds'

The air, singing in the winds,
the quietly chirruping ear of wheat,
the waters, and the whistling flame
all have their distinct voice.
But how can you catch the harmony
of the meadows where there are grasses and branches
and all the curves and modulations
of the noiseless, silent earth?

Her language is vague as patches,
her hot lips are mute,
her songs and long poems
are comprehensible only to the sensitive body.
She speaks with your body

in the tickling fallen wood in the thicket,
on the soft-dust covered road
and on the foot-path in the overrotten leaf.

Your body senses her, dying
with joy and enjoyment,
for in her is the power of primeval heaven
and the beating of the eternal heart.
Sometimes she compels sternly,
sometimes she kisses with hot lips and cares,
then she caresses with warmth and resilience
both your mother and your spouse.

Her silent waves,
her refrains and tales
flow together, filling the soul,
only into the narrow crack of touch.
Savour then through the mystery
of contact her revelation,
hidden in the wet and the dry land – listen
through your feet and through poems that have seen the light.

1950

In the Mist

A solitary sunset reached me here.
Who is caressing me? Who is calling me?
Only the tops of haystacks
float silently above the seas of mists.

In a cold field I hear the sound of springs.
The path drew me down
and now the blissfully fresh mist
envelops me.

In response my blood seethes
with this strange bursting joy
as if the soul of meadows and springs
grants me the gift of its love.

The haystacks intoxicate with their amazing fragrance,
every bush's dewdrops touch me like
the breath on someone's lips –
pearls on the dark skin.

Protecting us, silent and kind,
the gloom inclines towards us two.
I don't know how or why someone loves me,
I only sense that I am loved.

1950

Conclusion

Now my vagabond life for a half year
is concluded in the mists of snow.
The memory of lands that I have wandered over
on the earth cannot fit in my mind.

Those days when the skin of my feet
gently touched the soil and every track
was just a beginning,
like falling in love at sixteen.

Becoming used to the cool of the dew,
to the chilling frost,
I even stroll carefreely on the snow
and walk on the powdered glass of ice.

I am not a bridegroom visiting his fiancée
but a master in my family nest,
I put my feet wherever I want
because home for me is everywhere.

No joking. I repeat this again,
firm in my knowledge, there is truth in feelings
condemned by us to one side,
excluded from all arts.

But through these feelings, if the harmony
of consciousness can enter and sing with joy,
the music of creating the universe
will flow like a sound and a ray.

Your calling is to embrace much,
simple as a dove and wise as a snake,
so that your road would be laid
with purity and love of the elements.

The life-matter that stirs you will become
not a stagnant, dull veil
but a radiant, ringing Mass
with the dance of spirits by His feet.

This way knows no evil
nor the dispassionate sword of judgement.
Go and wander! Experience life! Try!
And then you will answer me: yes.

1935–1950
Trubchyovsk–Moscow–Vladimir

For Mishka the Bear

I loved him and I rocked him,
I comforted him in sadness;
he was absolutely white, and he grumbled
when he was laid on his back.

He sat the whole day on the little rug,
feigning stillness he would watch
the snowflakes outside the window
and the snow-covered roofs of the huts.

Fear could be read in his bead-eyes
and a light bewilderment
as if he had suddenly woken up
in an alien and unfamiliar village.

And the moment I intend to go out – he's here
with the heightened cunning of the beast:
he drinks in the freshness through the window
then silently peeps out from behind the door.

Whenever the netting in the white bed
protects us on all sides,
nestled down next to me, his warm body
may softly suddenly shiver in his sleep.

And lying curled up
I whisper, worried and shaking anxious:
Now, what is it Mishenka? what's up?
Sleep. It's time. Good night.

I have cherished in my faith,
like a tiny light beneath a snowy roof,
the certainty that in future paradise
we shall definitely be together with Mishka.

1950   [BC & RM]

Arseny Tarkovsky

(25 June 1907–27 May 1989)

Translated by Kitty Hunter Blair and by Richard McKane

ARSENY ALEXANDROVICH TARKOVSKY was born into a highly cultivated and original family. His father (journalist, banker and life-long political activist who spent some years in prison and exile under Alexander III) introduced him to poetry at a very early age. He started to publish poems in newspapers and journals in 1929; his first volume of verse was accepted for publication in 1946 and had reached proof stage when, in the aftermath of Zhdanov's infamous attack on Akhmatova and Zoshchenko, it was removed and destroyed because it 'lacked ideas'. His first published volume, *Before the Snow*, came out in 1962; eight more volumes followed, the last appearing in 1989. 'For decades', as his daughter Marina writes, 'he was part, and yet not part, of contemporary literature'. Until he was over fifty the general public knew him only as a masterly translator of poems from Arabic, Georgian, Armenian and Polish; also from Turkmenian, Azaerbaijani, Chechen, Ingush and Karakalpak. During the war he worked as a war correspondent, and in 1943 was gravely wounded and had to have a leg amputated.

He was married three times; his two children, Andrei (the film director) and Marina were by his first wife, Maria Ivanovna Vishniakova. All Andrei Tarkovsky's films are filled with reminiscences of his father's poems, whether by direct quotation or, more subtly, in images and motifs. Marina has written a beautiful episodic family chronicle entitled *Fragments of a Mirror*.

Arseny Tarkovsky was always held in high esteem by his fellow poets; when Anna Akhmatova was in England in 1965 he was the one 'real poet' whom she named in reply to a question about contemporary Soviet poetry. In official Soviet literary circles, however, he was criticized for his lack of ideological development, indeed, for the absence of ideology in his poems; and it is true that he was never a civic poet, the ethos of socialist realism was utterly alien to him. Poetry as he said was 'his very life'. His gift, as Sergei

Chuprinin has written, was that of seeing [a world in a grain of sand, / and a] 'Heaven in a Wild Flower', and he wrote of his vision with classical restraint, in reflective, philosophical tones. At every period, even in his dark poems about the war, his verse is marked by lyrical joy in nature. At every stage, too, there is deep pain, a sense of irrecoverable personal loss. 'Suffering is the constant companion of my life,' he said in 1982, 'I was only completely happy as a child'; and one remembers his wistful evocation of childhood, 'The Bright Day', with the repeated lines 'Never have I been / Happier than then'.

Marina Tarkovskaya tells us that from a folder of poems written in the 1950s, and numbered in Roman numerals, 156 had been removed, presumably by the poet himself. She argues convincingly that these poems were inspired by his unhappy love for a woman whose identity remains unknown. In an interview in 1982 Arseny Tarkovsky said that he had written more poems in 1952 than at any other time because that year had been a particularly unhappy one for him ('a totally happy person is unlikely to write poetry'). Of the poems that now remain from that decade, the great majority are from the latter years, above all from 1958.

Translation can preserve something of the poet's thought, and of his strong, original images; alas, virtually nothing can be conveyed of the finely honed rhymes and rhythms, haunting music and subtle correspondences.

Kitty Hunter Blair

Poets

We give stars in exchange for birds' clarinets
And flutes, for as long as the poets still live.
And the flutes in exchange for blue stamen brushes
For dragon-fly rattles and herdsmen's hide whips.

How strange to reflect that our barter has given
Us rhymes, in which there must be so much sorrow,
And voice, with its mixture of whistling and tin-plate,
In return for our own, root, underground honour.

And did you not love us and did you not praise us,
So why do you lie row on row in your graves,
And float on in silence, your coracles listing,
You – reaper, and psalmist, and carpenter prince?

1958   [KHB]

'Legacy belated'

Legacy belated,
Phantom, empty sound,
False mould of childhood
Pathetic native town.

Under weight of years
My shoulders are oppressed,
When all is said and done,
There's no point in this tryst.

It isn't the same sky
Seen now through the window,
Pale, bluish, smoky,
A white pigeon flying.

Sharply, far too sharply,
You can see from afar
A garish red curtain
In a window just ajar.

Not recognizing
Me as I go past
Stares the waxwork mask
Of years long gone by.

1955   [KHB]

'An eagle rests'

An eagle rests in the desolate steppe
On the blackened chimney of a burnt-out house.
So this is the pain that I've known since a child,
This bitter vision, as of Caesar's Rome –
Hunchback eagle, and no smoke, and no home . . .
This too, my heart, you have to bear.

1958   [KHB]

Ivan's Willow

Before the war Ivan walked by the stream;
A willow grew there, whose – no one knew.

No one knew why it spread over the stream;
Be that as it may – the tree was Ivan's.

In his tarpaulin, fallen in battle,
Ivan came back, below his own willow.

Ivan's willow tree,
Ivan's willow tree,
Like a white boat sails down the stream.

1958   [KHB]

Titania

Trunks stand erect in blessing,
There's milky vapour overhead.
I lie down on leaves of autumn,
Breathe in toadstool underwood.

My sinful earth, my innocent
Earth passes on to me
Her own ant-like tenacity,
Her soul's iodine strength.

My wanderings are at an end.
Into the labyrinth of roots
I'll go, Titania, find your throne,
lose myself in your domain.

What matter if my name be lost?
Your rusty leaf will be my shield.
Curse me, don't send me away,
Kill me, only let me stay.

1955   [KHB]

Blue-Tits

In the snow, while blue sky
                         looked green through branches
We stood on the path
                         and waited for a gift.

Blue-tits came flying,
                         stupendously noisy,
Sounding like silver spoons
                         in a Greek café.

It was just as if
                         out of nowhere
Blue sea was surging
                         up the white stones of a pier.

The waitress dropped crocks,
                         that skeetered on the floor,
The boss, bent double,
                         picked up spoons and swore.

1955   [KHB]

Insomnia

Furniture crackles at night.
Somewhere a pipe drips.
At this time shoulders are freed
From their daily load,
At this time things are given
Wordless human souls,
And blind
        mute
             deaf
They roam from floor to floor.
At this time city clocks
Despatch seconds
           hither
              and thither,
And they drag themselves along,
              lame,
                and halt.
Going up by lift,
            alive,
Not alive,
      or half alive,
Waiting in darkness where the water drips,
Taking glasses from their bags
And tripping a few gypsy dance steps,
Standing behind doors like disasters,
Slowly slipping drills into fittings,
At any moment now the wires will snap.
Actually they're more like the creditors
Come here for aye and ever,
Bringing bills,
         It's not possible
To pound water, on no sleep, in a mortar,
It's not possible to sleep, so restless
Is this night we were given just for rest.

1958   [KHB]

Song

My early years went by long ago,
Along the edge
Along the very edge
              of my own country
Over scythed mint, through blue heaven,
That heaven
          lost to me forever.

Rustling willow on the distant bank,
Like white hands.
The end of the bridge
             too far for me to walk.
But the moist sounds
           of that best name
I took as keepsake at our last good-bye.

She stands in the meander,
Washes white hands in the water,
And what I owe to her
            can not be paid.
I should say who stands
            in the water meadow,
On the distant bank,
Behind the willow, nymph-like
            above the river,
And flicks a ring over
           from finger to finger.

1960   [KHB]

Street Lamps

I remember the snow thaw
in that bitter early spring,
the drunk wind, lashing the face
on the run with icy sleet,
the restless proximity of nature
tearing through its white covering
and the ragged, noisy water
under the iron of sullen bridges.

What did you mean, what did you foretell,
street lamps under the cold rain,
and what sadnesses did you send
down on the city in your madness,
and wounded by what anxiety
and damaged by what hurt
from your lights is the city-dweller,
and how is he crushed and downcast?

Perhaps together with me
he is filled with the same anguish
and follows the leaden wave
avoiding the piers under the bridge?
He like I was deceived
by the secret dreams in your power,
so that it would be easier for us in July
to deny the black spring.

1951   [RM]

'On a black day'

On a black day I will dream
of a high star,
a deep well,
chill water
and the little crosses of lilac flowers
in dew so close to the eye.
But there are no more steps for us –
and the shadows will hide us.

If two people came out
from prison to freedom
they were you and I,
we are alone in the world
and we are no longer children
and am I not right
when your sleeve is brighter
than everything in the world?

Whatever will happen to us,
on my blackest day
I will dream on a black day
of a well and lilac,
a frail ring
and your simple dress –
and beyond the stream on the bridge
the wheels will clank.

All will pass in this world
and even this night
will pass and lead
you away from the garden.
Can we return this our dawn
into our power?
I look at my happiness
like a blind man.

A knock. 'Who's there?' 'Maria.'
The door opens: 'Who's there?'
No answer. The living
don't come to us like that,
their footsteps are heavier
and the hands of the living
are coarser and warmer
than your invisible hands.

'Where were you?' I hear
no answer to my question.
Perhaps my dream is
the scarcely heard clank of wheels
there on the bridge, beyond the stream
where the star is shining
and the frail ring has vanished
into the well for ever.

1952   [RM]

On the Bank

He was sitting by the river on the reeds
that had been scythed by peasants for roofs,
and it was quiet there and his soul
was even calmer and quieter.
He kicked off his boots and when he put
his feet in the water, the water
started talking to him not understanding
that he didn't know its language.
He thought that water is deaf and dumb
and the dwelling place of sleepy fish is wordless,
that dragonflies hover above the water
and catch mosquitoes or horseflies,

that if you want to wash, you wash, to drink, you drink,
and that there is no other sense in water.
But truly the language of water was a miracle,
some sort of tale about one and the same thing
like starlight, the fleeting flash of mica,
like the foretelling of disaster.
There was something in it from childhood,
from not being used to measuring life in years
and from something that has no name,
that comes at night before dreams,
from the threatening, growing
sensation of self in early years.

That was what the water was like that day
and its speech without sense or meaning.

1954   [RM]

'There is a smell of iron'

There is a smell of iron, of rotting potato,
of camp dust and salted sprats.
Where is your name, where are your wings?
the monster Viy bristles his moustache over Russia.

Who are you now? No cross, not a prayer.
the raft flounders on the deep river,
black sky above and kneaded clay
of the half-cooked bread in the hand.

He says: 'Lift my eyelids!'
He points at the settlements with his iron finger,
he marks down the rusty earth and the crippled elms
and starves them into a great fast.

He says: 'Lift my eyelids!'
If you don't you'll die for a trifle.
Dyrbala-arbala, dyrbala-arbala,
what else he's muttering you can't understand.

He ties sinews alive in a knot,
he plays cards with the taiga scurvy,
the hard frost rushes over the wormwood,
he'll fling you into the ravine, and adieu, my friend.

1946–1956   [RM]

VIY: folkloric monster, the title and subject of a story by Gogol. By
coincidence the Russian for 'wormwood' is *chernobyl*.

Paul Klee

Once upon a time there lived a painter called Paul Klee
somewhere beyond the mountains, over the meadows.
He sat down alone in an alley
with different-coloured pencils,

drew rectangles and little hooks,
Africa, a child on a platform,
a little devil in a pale blue shirt,
the stars and beasts on the horizon.

He did not want his drawings to be
an honest passport of nature
where people, houses, towns and waters
stand obediently in line.

He wanted streaks and stains,
like grasshoppers in the July heat,
to talk in fusion not confusingly.
And one morning a wing and the crown of a head

showed through on the card:
the angel of death began to take shape.
Klee realized that the time had come
to say farewell to his Muse and friends.

Klee said farewell and died.
There could be nothing more sad.
If Klee had been a bit fiercer
the angel of death would have been more natural.

Then together with the painter
we would all have disappeared from the world,
the angel would have shaken our bones.
But tell me why do we need that?

It's worse in the country churchyard than in the museum
where sometimes you living wander around
and Klee's paintings hang in a row,
blue, yellow, blissful.

1957   [RM]

Aeschylus

Embracing youth, I hastily
recoiled from my father's inheritance
and did not notice the omen that Aeschylus'
tragedy had weaved a nest in my poems.

Almost touching the beak and talons,
deceived by the thousand-year-old fable,
I played with fire like Prometheus
until I collapsed on the Caucasus mountains.

The messenger of the gods, a boy, a lackey
on the wings of one flitting over the stage,
'Look', I beg, 'here is my blood and bone,
go, take what you want – even the universe!'

No one from the chorus will save me,
will shout: 'Spare him or finish him off!'
and always every poem, resounding for more than a day,
lives under the same torture as Prometheus.

1959   [RM]

'You who lived before me'

You who lived before me on this earth,
my defenders and blood relatives,
from Dante to Sciaparelli,
thank you – you burned strong.

But don't I too burn strong
and do I dispassionately reproach
you, for whom I lived on earth so long,
grass and stars, butterflies and children?

I should take off my hat to you also
my city which
            is all like a notebook for writing music,
not yet touched by inspiration,
until July with a roar of kettle-drums rolls
down stone steps into the river,
until the pen boils over and fuses with the hand . . .

1959   [RM]

Joan of Arc's Tree

They talk to me, but I no longer hear
what they are saying. My soul heeds
only itself, and the voices sing to me
like those Joan of Arc heard.
I've learned how to control them:
I can call up the flutes, the bassoons,
the harps. Sometimes I wake
and everything is a distant echo
and the finale is this side of the mountain.

Hello, tall trunk and springy branches
with rusty-green leaves;
the mysterious tree from which
the bird's first note flies down to me.

I'm just about to grab a pencil
to write down in words the thunder of the kettledrums,
the hunting calls of the horn section,
the spring dashes of showers of the violins –
then I understand what is going on:
my soul puts a finger to my lips:
'Be quiet! Be quiet!'
All that makes death live
and life difficult, takes on a new,
manifest, transparent as glass,
sudden sense. And I am silent, but I
am left with nothing, just as I am
in the bell-shaped mouth of a funnel
full of the noise of the morning.

This is why, when we die,
it turns out that we never wrote
a single word about ourselves
and that which seemed to us to be us
goes in a circle,

calmly, estranged, outside comparison
and no longer contains us within itself.
Oh Joan, Joan, little Joan!
What gain is there in your king
being crowned? The magic oak rustles
and a voice says something, and you burn
in the flames in a shirt that's too big.

1959   [RM]

Socrates

I don't want either power over people
or honours or victories in war.
Just let me set like resin in a pine tree:
my origins are different: I'm no king.

It is given to you too, who drink my hemlock,
to taste dumbness and deafness.
I have not slave's rags on my back.
I am not alone – we are still in the future.

I am flesh of your flesh, the heights
of all earth's mountains and the depths of the sea.
Emptiness flooding the world
as a shell roars like Mount Olympus.

1959   [RM]

'Let Vincent van Gogh forgive me'

Let Vincent van Gogh forgive me
for my not being able to have helped him,

for not having strewn grasses
under his feet on the burning road,

for not having undone the laces
of his dusty peasant boots,

for not having given him water in the midday heat,
and that I did not stop him from shooting himself in the
     hospital.

Here I stand, and above me
a cypress looms twisted like a flame.

Lemon, chrome yellow and dark blue –
without them I would never have become myself;

I would have debased my own poetry
if I had thrown down another's burden.

And this roughness of an angel
that relates his brushstroke to my line

leads you too through the depth of his eye
to where Vincent breathes the stars.

1958

[RM]

In the Museum

We are not the Assyrians, they are:
those who have grasped with their claws the sceptre of state,
they are the clay-bearded gods, murderers of the people,
with their stiff royal clothes.

Blood, like a cobblestone, sticks out of the pitted throat,
and it's impossible to feel surfeited with life
when the feathered augur is thrust into the lion's chest
and the royal judgement's coarse vinegar stings the slaves'
    nostrils.

I curse the tiara of Shamshiadad.
Come whatever, I will never write his praises in cuneiform.
I do not need honour or bread on this earth
if I can't smash these royal wings.

Life is short, but one hundred of my lives would be enough
to fill the abyss that swallows bones.
I would have feasted well at the funeral feast
with those executed in the towered city of the Assyrians.

I damn the soles of the king's sandals.
Who am I? A lion or a slave, that my muscles
without recompense, should trample
the rectangular, stone ants into the salty earth.

1960   [RM]

Leonid Aronzon

(24 March 1939–13 October 1970)

Translated by Richard McKane

I CANNOT THINK of a more representative poet for the 1960s in any language than Leonid Aronzon. He has an internalized 'flower power', a mystic visionariness, a fertile visual imagination, a wild sense of humour; above all he is a love poet and the love poems are dedicated to his wife, Rita, whom he married in 1958. The couple were childless and in one poem he refers to Rita as his 'wife and daughter'. His landscapes are full of animals and flowers, butterflies, wild grasses, roses, sedge, mallows, trees; lakes, mountains, rivers, hills, rain, the sky turning from pale blue to dark blue. It is rather like those elegies of Peter Levi (one of Aronzon's first readers in English, and an admirer of his work) where the landscapes are depopulated but are in a riot of nature: surely there is an echo of Boris Pasternak in both these poets?

Leonid Aronzon was born in Leningrad/Petersburg and lived there all of his life. Many of his poems add to the panoply of poems written in that city, which in the 1960s was teeming with poetry. Viktor Krivulin has recently advanced the theory that Aronzon was then a rival of equal standing to Brodsky. Anna Akhmatova was still alive; Nayman, Bobyshev, Rein (on her death soon to be called together with Brodsky 'Akhmatova's orphans'), Kuzminsky, Kushner, Krivulin, Volokhonsky, and Krasovitsky (in Moscow) were all writing. Elena Shvarts, one of my favourite living Russian poets, was starting her career – an excellent bilingual book of her poems, translated by Michael Molnar, *Paradise*, is published by Bloodaxe Books. She was also to edit a book of Aronzon. *Samizdat* in pre-photocopier days – typewriters primed with three carbon copies – was in full swing, along with poetry cafés like 'Saigon'. Aronzon did not publish a single poem of his own in his lifetime except for some children's poems.

There are treasures in early Aronzon, who was influenced first by the Acmeists (Akhmatova, Mandelstam, Gumilyov), then there is the influence of the Futurist Velimir Khlebnikov, then the OBERIU, Nikolay Zabolotsky, who has recently been translated by Daniel Weissbort, more than Kharms and Vvedensky. Aronzon had written his doctoral thesis at Leningrad University on Zabolotsky.

Aronzon taught Russian Literature for a time but his main job was as a film-script writer for scientific (this word is broader in Russian) films. He contracted osteomyelitis in 1960 on an expedition to north-east Russia, but a series of operations was successful. His early death, near Tashkent, most probably by suicide, is always zeroed in on by commentators. On a recent trip to the USA I met Vitaliy Aronzon, Leonid's older brother, who showed me archive materials of Aronzon, including two letters from Rita to Larissa Haikina, which express concern and alarm about her husband's mindset around the time of his death. Suffice it to say that Aronzon shot himself in the stomach with a shotgun he had come across in a shepherd's hut in the mountains. His friend Altshuler found him by a haystack. Rita's great friend Irena Orlova wrote to me: 'His suicide was not an act of desperation, more a dramatic act, an experiment, a desire to experience something like it, to wound himself slightly, to grasp how it is. He missed. God is very hard on poets and experimenters . . . '

There are intense mood-swings in Aronzon's poetry. Larissa Miller in her review of my bilingual book *Death of a Butterfly: Poems of Leonid Aronzon*, published by Gnosis in Moscow and Diamond Press in London, indicates some of the conflicting emotions and juxtapositions. In a prose poem, writing about his uncle, whose son had recently died, Aronzon says: 'The swings,' Uncle said, 'carried me up to the highest joy and dropped me to the limits of despair. Sometimes such a swing would stretch out for months, sometimes it lasted a few seconds, but every time the extreme situation seemed to be final.'

Aronzon was a discovery for this translator who started working on him five years after his death. I trust that readers will find in him not only the spirit of the 1960s, but also a survivor poet for the 21st century.

I would like to thank Victoria Andreyeva, Arkady Rovner, Felix and Max Jacubson, Vitaliy Aronzon, Irena Orlova and Geoffrey Godbert. Some of these translations have been published in *Stand*, *Acumen*, *Index* and *Poet for Poet* (Hearing Eye).

Richard McKane

Pavlovsk

The twilight is already like rain.
Wet Pavlovsk, autumnal Pavlovsk,
flies all over, around, trembles
and stutters like a candle.
O August,
will you bury me like the grass
preserving the fallen leaves,
or a fox's soft track
leading me back to the capital?

There is jaundice of street lamps in this autumn
and the ornamental ceilings plunge in, swim.
Come then, my death, in October
on platforms washed out as faces,
but not here, where the trees are tsars,
where the death of decay rules,
where the last bird soars
and the midnight light slithers down the steps
like a leaf and lies down,
where the oak, like an unrecognized contemporary,
shakes each branch,
dwelling, as before, in immortality.

Here I am tsar, I am alone,
hence like an actor who has warmed up
I let myself slide like the rains
and settle on the ground as leaves,
and the palace night among the nests
lavishes the lingering August
with an infinity of shooting stars
over exposed and gloomy Pavlovsk.

1961

'To break on words'

To break on words spears sharpened on mania:
in every black envy there is an imperishable thirst for likeness,
in every thing and every dream there is an unparalleled lust.
Here is the stream over the leaves. Let's talk about the stream.
Here is the stream over the leaves. It is the early moisture and
    light.
I look at you, reflected in the wild grass.
To wake, but why? In your dream you lean over the stream,
I will never teach you anything till death comes.
Oh, shake like a leaf, and holding on to a branch, lean over,
sliding down the grass as you fall, catching onto the grass.
O language of reflection, O tongue torn out at the root,
you repeat painfully the ABC learned by someone parrot-fashion.
Here is the stream over the leaves. Lean over it holding your
    breath.
The wordless embryo beating under your heart is still the same
    soul.
Here is the stream over the leaves. And over it the clouds, clouds,
and your exhausted hand sliding through the grass again.
Horses will wander, heads lowered and look into the stream.
So bury your face in your hands and listen to your death
    approaching.

1962–63

Song

You hear the water slapping
up and down the bottom, the sides of the boat,
when those two giving themselves over
to the rocking of the waves,

lie like the dead, turning
their faces to the peace of the skies
and the morning sand breathes,
bumped by boats into the reeds.

When I, your dear one, die,
forget the ceremonial,
leave me lying in the pine-wood
with a face like these lakes!

1963

Message to the Clinic

Draw my name on the sand in the overcast park, as though
    by candlelight,
and live through till summer, to weave wreaths, that the
    stream will carry away.
It meanders through the saplings, drawing my name on the
    sand
as with the withered stick which you are holding now in
    your hand.
The grass is high here, and the pale blue lakes are lying like
    mirrors
of the calm, slow skies, rocking the doubled forest,
while the cigarette-paper wings of blue dragonflies vibrate
    sleepily.
You walk by the stream, dropping flowers, looking at
    rainbow fish.
The flowers are heavy with nectar, and the stream is writing
    my name
and forming landscapes: now a backwater, now a reach.
Yes, we'll lie here, and you hear the grass growing through
    me.

Sewn onto the earth, I see the sleepy dragonflies and hear only
    words:
perhaps the woods round murky lakes are the sum of our life:
the chirring of dragonflies, a plane, a quiet reach and
    interlacement of flowers
are that soul's space, in which are hills and lakes; here are
    horses running,
and the forest ends and you walk on the wet sand beside the
    stream, dropping flowers.
Flute music follows you, swarms of butterflies, life follows you,
they all call you as they accompany you, as you walk by the
    stream and no one is with you.
The light on everything is smooth, young from the
    neighbouring lakes,
as though, in the distance, a luminous, high cathedral were
    constructed out of the autumn sky;
if it's not there, then tell me for the Lord's sake, why is
a peaceful, unhurrying, muddy stream meandering like you
    through the saplings drawing my name,
and the plane flying over the lake on this hot day is reading it?
Perhaps the stream is not a stream, but my name alone.
So, look at the grass in the mornings, when the slow steam
    spreads,
alongside is the light of street lamps, light of buildings, and
    your leafless park is all around,
where you draw with the withered stick a chance, unhurrying
    and muddy stream
that carries off wreaths of nectar-bearing flowers, and the reed
    butterflies
sit on your shoulder and the blue dragonflies are all around,
and you walk by the stream, dropping flowers, looking at
    rainbow fish,
and the rain sketched by me breaks out of the sheet music,
you draw the stream, beside which you walk and walk
    afterwards.

April 1964

'Having bent thought to hang it up'

Having bent thought to hang it up like a horseshoe
I will clothe all living things in words,
and giving it to you to learn by heart
I will lounge in the armchair of some delta.

1965

'Not this but another silence'

Not this but another silence,
like a horse leaping up to God
I want to lay down sound
with my thoughts and style from end to end,
I want to die young
in the hope: that I'll maybe arise again
not totally, perhaps a third of me,
for just a day, oh such a wonderful day.
The stream of Lesbos water
turns the mill-wheel
and a young girl sees someone's dreams
after they were slowly sung,
O body: sun, dream, stream!
The cathedrals of autumn are tall,
when I lie on the sedge of three lakes
I am God's and nobody's.

1966?

Sonnet in Igarka

For Al. Altshuler

Our nights are whiter with you,
that means the whole world is whiter,
whiter than swans
and a cloud and daughters' necks.

What is nature? A literal translation
of the languages of heaven? And Orpheus
is not the poet, not Orpheus,
but Gnedich, Kashkin, a translator?

And really, just where is the sonnet there?
Alas, it doesn't exist in nature.
It has woods, but not the Tree:

it is in the gardens of non-existence:
and Orpheus flattering Eurydice
was singing of Eve rather than Eurydice.

June 1967

'My wife's body – from spring to spring'

My wife's body – from spring to spring,
I lie next to it in the lofty silence.
Night will only end at midday
by the tree next to the wall.

The tree with the night and the night with the tree
stand alongside, exactly repeating each other,
my wife, daughter of the night and the tree.
will wake up only at midday.

I reached out to the leaves
to strew the alcove with flowers.

Summer 1967

Aronzon's Vision

Beginning of a Long Poem

Frost in the deserted skies,
the number of immortals has sunk to the depths
but the angel on duty bears the chill,
dodging the shallow stars.

And in the room my wife's face,
with her luxuriant hair, is pale on the pillow,
my wife's face and her eyes
and on her body two wonderful breasts.

I kiss her face at the temple.
There's such a frost outside: I can't hold back the tears.
I have fewer and fewer friends among the living
and more and more among the dead.

Snow illuminates the beauty of your faces
and the space in my soul,
and with each kiss I am saying farewell . . .
The candle burns, I am carrying it

to the top of the hill, the snowy mound.
A glance at the skies. The moon was still yellow,
dividing the hill into a black slope and a white one,
on the white side the pine-woods stretched.

Fresh snow lay on the rough crust.
Here and there the sedge thrust through.
Those woods were indistinguishable
on the dark side. The moon shone aslant.

Exemplifying the vagaries of somnambulism
I climbed, raising the shadows,
and forced onto my knees by the summit
smoothly thrust the candle into the splendour of the snow.

January 1968

'It's good to stroll along in heaven'

It's good to stroll along in heaven,
what a heaven, and what is beyond it?
I never ever was
so handsome, so enchanted.

The body moves without support,
naked Juno is all around
and the non-existent music
and an uncomposed sonnet.

It's good to stroll along in heaven,
barefoot for better exercise.
It's good to stroll along in heaven
reciting Aronzon out loud.

Spring, morning, 1968

Poem Written in Expectation of Awakening

The fauna frolics in the flora
trampling and eating it,
and on a hill sits Danaea.
This is why eyes mist over
and anguish is all around
because this young girl is
fornicating with the hill.

May, morning, 1968

Forgotten Sonnet

Sleeplessness all day. Sleeplessness since morning.
Sleeplessness till evening. I walk
around the circle of rooms. They're all like bedrooms.
Sleeplessness is everywhere. It's time for me to sleep.

If I'd died yesterday
today I would be happy and sad,
but I wouldn't be sorry for living in the beginning . . .
But I'm alive: my flesh has not died.

Six more lines, which don't exist yet,
I'll drag out of preexistence into a sonnet
not knowing what this torture is for.

Why do such thoughts and letters
blossom in bouquets from corpses of souls?
But I evoked them – and let them live.

A day in May 1968

'Scented eruption'

Scented eruption, spreading lava of flowers flooded hill:
but breaking off the bliss that comes is not in one's powers.
From every pore springs burst forth, springs of flowers and the
    glory of God
and a metaphor of a butterfly flies high as exhalation of the
    lava's steam-cloud.

May 1968

'There is silence between everything'

There is silence between everything. One.
One silence. A second, a third.
full of silences. Each of them is:
the material for a network of poems.

And a word is the thread. Pass it through
the needle and you make a window with word-threads –
now silence is framed
and it is a mesh in the sonnet's net.

The bigger the mesh, the larger
the dimensions of the soul that's caught up in it.
However abundant the catch it will be less

than that of the fisherman, who is bold enough
to make so gigantic a net
that it would have but a single mesh.

1968

Sonnet to the Soul and Corpse of N. Zabolotsky

There is an easy gift – as if for a second
happy time it repeats experience.
(The tropes of images and metaphors of the lofty rivers
raised by the mountain are light and flexible.)

But I am allotted a different gift:
at times poems are a whisper of exhaustion
and I do not risk Pushkin's rhyme for Europe,*
let alone come to terms with the game.

Work, alas, will always be shameful
where roses, getting prettier, are blooming
and breathing sound into the reed-pipes

of their clarinets, drums, trumpets
all make music – plants and beasts
with the roots of souls breaking up the corpse.

Evening, May 1968

* Pushkin, in a poem 'Refutatsiya g-na Beranzhera', 1827, rhymes
'Evropa' (there aren't that many rhymes for it in Russian) with
'jopa' (arse): a rhyme which Aronzon, who rhymes mellifluously
throughout his poems, wisely eschews.

Two Identical Sonnets

I

My love, sleep, my little golden one,
dressed all in satin skin.
I seem to think we've met somewhere:
I know your nipple so well and your underwear.

How it suits you, how it goes with you, it's just you:
all this day, all this Bach, all this body,
this day, and this Bach, and this plane
flying there, flying here, flying somewhere.

Into this garden, into this Bach, into this moment,
fall asleep, my love, fall asleep without covering up:
your sacred face and bottom, bottom and crotch, crotch and
        face,
let all sleep, let all sleep, my living one.

Not approaching one iota, not one step,
give yourself up to me in all gardens and conjugations.

II

My love, sleep, my little golden one,
dressed all in satin skin.
I seem to think we've met somewhere:
I know your nipple so well and your underwear.

How it suits you, how it goes with you, it's just you:
all this day, all this Bach, all this body,
this day, and this Bach, and this plane
flying there, flying here, flying somewhere.

Into this garden, into this Bach, into this moment,
fall asleep, my love, fall asleep without covering up:

your sacred face and bottom, bottom and crotch, crotch and
    face,
let all sleep, let all sleep, my living one.

Not approaching one iota, not one step,
give yourself up to me in all gardens and conjugations.

1969

'Nature all around'

Nature all around
was metaphorical:
there stood a wicked-tree
in which, O Lord, a bird lived.
When the bird died
a crowd of people gathered there:
`Let's go off flying round the kichen-garden!'
They went off flying round and jumped, then what?
This is what this noble evening's for,
and the lilac and the butterflies too!

Summer 1969

'Alas I'm alive. Deathly dead'

Alas I'm alive. Deathly dead.
Words are filled with silence.
The gift rug of nature I rolled up
into a primordial roll.

In front of all nights I lie,
staring at them.
Glenn Gould, the pianist of my fate,
plays with note signs.

Here is the consolation for my melancholy
but it brings more dread.
Thoughts are swarming but not meeting.

An airy rootless flower,
here is my tame butterfly.
Here is my life – what can I do with it?

November 1969

Empty Sonnet

Who loved you more rapturously than I?
May God protect you, God protect you, O God protect you.
The gardens wait, the gardens wait, wait in the nights
and you in the gardens, you in the gardens are waiting too.

I would like to, I would like to instil my sadness
into you, instil it so as not to alarm
your sight of the night grass, your sight of its stream,
so that sadness, so that grass would become our bed.

To pierce into the night, to pierce into the garden, to pierce
    into you,
to lift eyes, to lift eyes to compare the night in the garden
with the heavens, and the garden in the night, and the garden
which is full of your night voices.

I go towards them. Face full of eyes,
the gardens are waiting for you to wait in them.

1969

'The wall is full of shadows'

The wall is full of shadows
of the trees. (Dot, dot, dot.)
I woke at dead of night:
life is given, but what can one do with it?

I was allowed into heaven *in absentia*
and flew to it in my dream,
but I woke at dead of night:
life is given, but what can one do with it?

Although the nights are longer and longer,
twenty-four hours is still twenty-four hours.
I woke at dead of night:
life is given, but what can one do with it?

Life is given, but what can one do with it?
I woke at dead of night.
O, my wife, in reality
you are beautiful as in a dream.

1969

'Am I here? But my God is by my side'

Am I here? But my God is by my side
and it's easy for me to say to him:
'Oh, how beautiful is the boundlessness
and the solitude of everything!'

Wherever time may flow
I don't care. I can see joy,
but in my not needing it
it's hard for me even to dream.

Yet as morning breaks
I like to raise an eyelid
to look at you, my friend,
to look at my God and think thus:
'Who could stamp on my wing
when You are my protector?'

1969–1970

'Oh my God, how beautiful it all is'

Oh my God, how beautiful it all is!
Every time, as never before.
There is no break in the beauty.
Shall I turn away? But where to?

The trembling wind is cool
because it comes off the river.
There's no world behind –
everything is before me!

Spring 1970

'My beauty, my goddess, my angel'

My beauty, my goddess, my angel,
the source, estuary of all my thoughts,
you are my stream in summer, my fire in winter.
I am happy that I lived to see that spring
when you appeared before me
in your sudden beauty.
I knew you as whore and saint
loving all I recognized in you.
I don't want to live in tomorrow, but in yesterday,
so that life should track back to our beginning
in the time we have left together
and roll out again if the years allow.
But since we are going to live on further
and the future is a cruel desert,
you are the oasis that will save me,
my beauty, my goddess.

1970

'Outside the window'

Outside the window are the night and the frost.
I look out through the gap.
And you are sitting, my wife and daughter,
not hiding your breast.

You are sitting happily in your beauty
as if in long ago days,
when your longing
had nothing to do with the body.

Your sadness was free
of fetters and flesh:
no words were needed to express it –
it was just the vast distance.

And in this morning distance
there already appeared
like a wonderful garden
the peaks and heavens of the earth.

You were dissolved
in the world space.
Waves had not yet turned to foam
and you were all around.

You were the breath of a winged beast.
You were his water in a river
and you were so beautiful,
beautifully unformed.

Since those times, I believe,
from those very sorrows,
there remained in you some groan
and a body with its beauty.

That is why I shut the hole in the window,
I go to my divan
where you are sitting not hiding your breast
and all your other ecstasies.

1969–1970?

'It flickers – then nothing'

It flickers – then nothing.
Death of a butterfly? The candle flame?
The hot wax streams
over my arm and shoulder.

I raise the candle over my memory
and fly, fly astride my lady.
(What a butterfly you are!)
I fly to see death.

Then she flies on me
and I light the way.
What a huge breast she has!
How quiet it is in the dark silence.

Everywhere is as in the soul:
it's not yet August, but it's over.

1970

'How good it is in abandoned places'

How good it is in abandoned places,
abandoned by men but not the gods.
It's raining: the beauty of the ancient groves
raised on hills is soaked.

It's raining: the beauty of the ancient groves
raised on hills is soaked.
We're alone here, no people are our equals.
Oh, how blessèd it is to drink in the mist.

We're alone here, no people are our equals.
Oh, how blessèd it is to drink in the mist.
Remember the path of the fallen leaf
and the idea that we go on after us.

Remember the path of the fallen leaf
and the idea that we go on after us.
Who rewarded us, my friend, with these dreams
or did we give ourselves this reward?

Who rewarded us, my friend, with these dreams
or did we give ourselves this reward?
To shoot oneself here one needs no devil:
nor aching in the soul, nor powder in the gun.

Nor even a gun. God sees that
to shoot oneself here one needs nothing.

September 1970

Anonymous poet from
the Arsenal Mental Prison Hospital

Translated by Richard McKane

IN EVERY ANTHOLOGY there should be a poet who doesn't quite fit. The unknown poet from the Leningrad Arsenal Mental Prison Hospital is such. In the mid-seventies I met the dissident Victor Fainberg and the psychiatrist who saved his life, Marina Voikhanskaya, at an Index on Censorship party. CAPA (Campaign against Psychiatric Abuse), or 'Capitolina Ivanovna' as Victor dubbed it, was formed and I was happy to work alongside Victor and Marina, the late David Markham, the redoubtable Max Gammon, William Shawcross, the late George Theiner of *Index*, James Thackara, Tom Stoppard, Lord Avebury and others. We campaigned for the mathematician Leonid Plyushch, Anatoly Shcharansky, the poet Zinovy Krasivsky and many more, and of course Vladimir Bukovsky. In those years *glasnost*, cleverly lifted by Gorbachev in the 1980s, meant 'publicity for a cause'. Victor told me that he had been given in Arsenal a little book, bound in elasto-plast, containing about one hundred poems written in a regular but difficult-to-decipher hand. The man who gave it to him was a 'thief of honour' and claimed to have clandestinely written out the poems in one night and that they were by many hands (which seems unlikely). The poems do not rhyme. I translated them all in the seventies. I took the precaution of having the poems deciphered and typed out by a Russian friend: this stood me in good stead when ten years later I lost the book in the confusion of my own admission to a hospital in London. However, I do still have photo-copies of some pages of the original. *Gnosis*, the magazine pub-lished by Arkady Rovner and Victoria Andreyeva, printed some poems and translations under the pseudonym of Ivan Bulyzhnikov (John Cobblestone), and *The Month*'s editor, the late Hugh Kaye, printed my translations in two issues. Two poems were printed in *Beyond Bedlam* (Anvil Press) and a dozen in my *Poet for Poet* (Hearing Eye).

Victor thought that the poems might be by a poet or poets who were 'genuinely mentally ill' – which he was not. I tend to think that the poems are by one hand. The Arsenal was used as a punitive psychiatric hospital for dissidents. Massive doses of Aminazine (chlorpromazine / largactil), known as 'the liquid cosh'), and the punishment drug Sulfazine (which violently raises the temperature) were regularly used.

The images are strong, with a suppressed anger and escapism. The love poems are anguished. The poems' mysterious origin adds to their effect and they are representative of a significant segment of life and poetry in Russia in the 1970s. The feelings of incarceration are authentic. If the Unknown Mental Patient has survived somewhere in Russia or wherever I would like to return to him his poems – with interest, for he gave them to Victor in the hospital when he knew that he might go to the West.

Richard McKane

'Round the globe the train of dust'

Round the globe the train of dust,
round the globe the dust of mirages,
the shadow on the globe turns black,
the globe in the shadows of lost days.

The emerald sky has stretched out
over the planet of maddened shadows,
towers have thrust their voice into the heavens
and exploded in the chaos of steps.

The chain swings on the wall
like the pendulum of an antique clock,
and I am in my mad fire
of voices half-sane as the day.

'In the humpbacked Arbat streets'

In the humpbacked Arbat streets
an alien man got lost.
Much seems to him to be strange
in the noisy autumn peoplelessness.

The street lamps and shop windows in a torrent
of rusty light splash in the dark
and the windows of people's thoughts, of beasts
look at the autumn night.

Noisy crowds rush past
in the howling of the cold wind
and the desert of the autumn peoplelessness
is bloodsucked with the hubbub of greed.

In the humpbacked backstreets of the Arbat
an alien man got lost –
he is like a beast captive in a bestiary
and does not find the way out of the cage.

'On the gloomy horizon of the cell'

On the gloomy horizon of the cell
no hope of the star's shining –
only a sun yellow like sardines
and the dull waiting – when?

Waiting surrounded the cell
like a ghost of dead minutes,
it's the years of pains and distances,
I walk in delirium I fly in delirium.

On the gloomy horizon of the cell
no hope of the stars leaving a track.
Unhappiness menacingly rules in the cell
with a station change for the other world or this world.

This cell – the delirium of my fantasy,
if I am a ghost among people,
this cell is a door to the expanse of the Odyssey,
the voices and wishes of the people.

'The night whirled'

The night whirled.
The tired day's sun
like a man's soul
has set.
Shadows have come alive,
ghosts wander in the graveyards of twilight.

The dark night's suns in the whirlpool of the sky
galloped helter-skelter and disappeared
and songs rang out like a thousand bells,
sweeping away the tracks of the caravan.

The heart suddenly hurried
to the full refectory table
and thoughts soared in the round dance.

Cherishing the misty distance
as hope for a meeting,
the trains exchanged greetings
from their distant night wanderings
and
a new world of alarming waitings
arose stunningly.
The steps clambered up
to the sky's extreme
and set
like night suns
in dawn partings.

The boomerang of memory

The boomerang of memory
hurtles into consciousness
like the Red Indian's arrow
with a poisoned tip,
kills, wounds,
gives birth to frenzy,
with hope for the past
to the madness of the ultimate,
with a bloody dotted line
of burnt out thoughts,
couples emptiness
and the miracle with the world,
and my shadow steals
up the steps
of a huge staircase
        from the cobweb of days.
That same boomerang
hurtles into consciousness
and I am a Red Indian,
but my arrow
flies past the mark today . . .

In the sands of the desert
the caravan has disappeared,
burdened with the burden of memory,
amen.

'Don't come to me'

Don't come to me,
it's difficult for me to talk with you.
I cannot love you
and it's not in me to give you
the breath of joy.
Don't come to me.

The years have closed tight shut,
in the abyss of terrible distances
the flamelets of desires have died.
You have become a memory deceived,
you are somewhere there,
the years have closed tight shut.

Don't come to me.
I shall not return to your crystal world.
You are the distant echo of a song.
You were for me,
          but became
that which one loses without finding.
Don't come to me.

'Free steps have finished'

Free steps have finished.
A new world has risen:
alarm,
the dust of doubts,
the bell chimes float
on the fallen asleep world.
The eternal 'forgive',
the groan of black thirst,

the torture of lips calling over me,
of dear eyes
and the flame of the old secret.
(This isn't accidental,
this only happens once in a lifetime.)
I have gone through everything,
but alone
I cannot find
what I found over the grey water.
And, my God, I will hear
so many angry words
of faithlessness
to God
which you perhaps will never say to me.
But
all the steps
are at the threshold.
Once upon a time
I loved.

'Again the drops of red-brown liquor'

Again the drops of red-brown liquor,
again
raindrops
beat
on the windowpanes.
Again the mountain air of Daghestan.
Again your echo
close
beside me.

But when will these
disappear at last:
this table

this pain
this abyss
and the constellations of arms
intertwine
and the mists of parting
will melt
and I will see the whirlpools of your eyes
and fill them with the sun's happiness?

Raindrops again
beat on the windowpanes.
Come to me
my distant happiness.

'As a man always returns'

As
a man always returns
to the places he has fallen in love with
which have subconsciously and imperceptibly
become a part of himself
(for some it's the sea,
another livens up among the expanse
and green giants of the taiga,
another one can only breathe
freely in the mountains);
so I always return
to the world of the already familiar
but always surprisingly new,
now urgent, now peaceful
many-meaning concepts and images.
I meet you –
the sign of trouble,
the smile of the dawn,
the sea's waves,

the secret thought,
the sun, the idea.
You are the universe's breathing,
my unattainable sphinx,
sadness and the storm.
You,
I call fabled
creatures unlike
each other.
Thus I call the light of dawn,
the footsteps of thought
and the sparkle of creation,
the thousand-namedness of those forms
I give up to one meaning.
I combine thousands of meanings into a form
and I search for you.

'When the sun dissolves'

When the sun dissolves over the vault of the sky
in a torn hieroglyph of breathing
and in the commotion of fiery stripes
the fireworks of waterfalls thunder –

on the black break of centuries,
like a mainspring of abstract anger
the scales of hallucination sparkle
and on the horizon of roads
in the green boiling of [*illegible word*]
the cone of eternity soars.

'The mole strayed'

The mole strayed into the green of the waves,
the peals of thunder shook the sieve.
The smoke of distant gullies arose
and floated like a transparent shroud.

The mist whirled into a column
under the greying, tired sky
and the caravan got lost in the expanses
and the paths were sprinkled with poems.

The song goes away with the caravan,
the song of the sky of the sands of the oceans.
Lava of snow flows from the mountains
and smashes to pieces like the roaring of a tiger.

'An unknown track flares'

An unknown track flares
on the wiped-out line on the horizon
(someone walked over the earth in the rain
and is continuing on his way in heaven).

The horizon
is the frontier of two worlds,
it's difficult to cross it today,
and tomorrow it will be absolutely impossible.

So one has to gather all one's strength
on the frontier of tomorrow and today
and to go away leaving between them
all that these two countries,

today – the present
and today – the tomorrow of the past,
compared you to,
throughout the many ages.

'In a blinded window'

In a blinded window
suddenly
the tunnel of the dawn along the staircase
appeared in all its definition
like footsteps hastening through sunny leaves
and everything fell tensely silent.
Rustles hid themselves,
the birds swallowed their voices,
the sun motionlessly spread its rays
and sunbeams rustled in the eyes.
And in this
fallen silent world
suddenly
a worried state came about
and the silent millstones of fortune-telling turned
and the universal waiting
replied
with a turquoise string in her soul
and she
came in and the numbed world
suddenly burst out with the wild enjoyment of sounds,
everything rang,
sparkled,
sparked,
the birds' trill welled up,
the sky sighed,
sun sparkles

came alive and leapt
and the wind whipped in the smoke of her hair.
She said
it is for ever.
And lips
burned,
attracted,
tortured,
and sliding over them
a snake
bit the world
and the morning
and fading the doubts of eyes
flowers fell from the ring of her hands
and scattered over her dress
and hands
swam in the ocean of the sky,
and she
swam over the earth
and the earth
swam in a flaring heat-haze.

'A mammoth'

A mammoth
whose outline has long been forgotten
scrambles out from under the ice onto the granite,
walks
into another epoch,
heavily, slowly,
looks around,
but
nowhere meets
any familiar pictures.

Under the huge bell of its skull
a thought passes.
The snake of horror penetrating into all
the corners of the being of the huge
monument of history.
He hears around him
only the echo
which fades with each moment.
He hears a soft whisper
but the whisper is enough.
The beast sees
and knows that he has appeared out of time
and also
that his times have passed.
His time has changed
for another
and in his predatorily curled tusks
oblivion weaved him a nest.
The ancient fragment doesn't understand
anything.
He isn't needed by anyone,
he is an echo
but there is something criminal living in him
and he goes off
before death for eternity,
but leaves nothing
except
the masses of his mirage,
whose entrance
is guarded by the sullen ice-ridges.

'I'm tired'

I'm tired,
tension needs to be relieved.
I need to change,
but
I'm tired.
They always put me in place
(perhaps because I'm weak
and so tired
they always put me in place . . .)
I'm a thing,
but I understand everything.
(A thinking thing –
I think that I'm not understood.
I engender sympathy to myself
and compassion.)
I need to change
but I'm . . .
Listen,
it's true you see,
I don't change.
(A thing thinks
tormentingly tries to remember
what beast it is like,
runs through close things familiar things:
crickets . . . cockroaches . . . spiders . . . a moth . . .)
No
everything is not right.
A thing wants the grandiose,
the huge relationship . . .
But I'm
a cupboard,
primitive, containing barytes.
I have already swallowed my maximum.
You look into the cupboard
and there . . . it's empty.

To you it seems that it's a complex mechanism
like a clock
or a man
but it's only an empty cupboard
(now it's an empty drawer
of some imitation perfume,
it smells of cheap soap
but it wants to smell of something expensive
and the drawers fling dust in the eyes . . .).
Or
it's the dull drumming,
it swaggers with its importance,
it's blown up and . . .
You wait for something unusual from it
but in the drumming physical laws
toss around,
rationalize . . .
I'm tired,
I would like to . . .
(Now you see a cockroach,
smoking smoke
with a pipe into the eyes.)
You think that I've changed,
you entertain doubts, you see.
Thoughts swarm
and buzz like a honeycomb
and a degrading terror.
(It turns out it's not a cockroach but a millipede
. . . one is no better than the other.)
Everything stifling.
I'm a thing.
They'll put me in place now
with regret.
(You think I don't understand.)
I'm tired
and I need to change,
only
I don't understand anything.

Someone will put me in place,
attending me
with sensitivity.
But . . .
But I'm a thing.
I fall and smash,
I smash.
I destroy all the efforts around me.
Tension needs to be relieved,
and I want to say in a
human way:
. . . I understand much.
. . . Don't put me in place.
I see everything.
I know what's required
of me.
But I can't do much.
. . . I'm simply tired.

Viktor Krivulin

(9 July 1944–17 March 2001)

Translated by Michael Molnar

VIKTOR KRIVULIN's work spans four decades but there is good
reason for assigning him the 1980s in this anthology. While the
Soviet system went from stagnation to *perestroika* to dissolution, his
work mapped out the situation of conscience and creativity strug-
gling against suppression or indifference. What might have seemed
an élitist predicament in another period now affected everyone.
Glasnost recognized the need for a new social order. *Gallery,* the
poem-cycle translated here, anticipated it by several years and, in
the guise of lyrical art criticism, the poems highlight the malaise
that made it necessary.

Krivulin spent most of his life in Leningrad/St Petersburg.
While still at Leningrad University, in 1967 he resigned from the
Komsomol. From then on any academic or official career was
closed. Instead he chose marginality, life in semi-poverty in com-
munal apartments and hectic artistic activity. He and his generation
grew up during the years of cultural isolation, conscious of having
to create their own parallel culture. From 1975 to 1981, together
with his wife Tatyana Goricheva, he edited the first *samizdat* jour-
nal devoted to literature, art, religious and cultural commentary –
37. During the early and mid-1980s Krivulin also participated in
the semi-official activities of 'Klub-81'. His first Soviet publication
was in the group's anthology, *Krug* (Leningrad, 1986), which
includes the 11th poem from the *Gallery* cycle. Meanwhile his
work continued to be published by the émigré press in Paris.

Under the Soviet system Krivulin and his generation lived in
'concealed freedom'. In the 1990s he adapted immediately to the
new environment by turning himself into a campaigner for demo-
cracy. He was vice-president of the St Petersburg PEN Club and
co-chairman of the St Petersburg branch of the Democratic Russia
party, where he worked for Galina Starovoitova, courageously
representing her party after she was assassinated in 1998. The

poetry continued, historical and geographical metaphors of Russia's fate. The latest collection I received (by e-mail), *Poems – 2000*, begins with 'The Din of Progress' and ends with 'Above the Rubbish Heap'.

Finally, a translator's note to explain the layout of the poems. 'One reads a typescript differently from a printed book' Krivulin wrote during his *samizdat* days and his own poems belong in this unofficial space. Reader and writer should meet on equal footing. The imagery of the *Gallery* cycle emerges from the contradictions between everyday life and art; its theme is the pathos of individuals tortured and deformed by impossible social demands. Each poem is preceded by a description of an image and the poem itself is a marginal annotation to the image. The factual footnotes were added by the poet at the translator's request, bearing in mind the necessity of contextualizing references obscure to a non-Soviet reader at the time (and now to the post-Soviet reader).

There is a further level of marginal commentary which is missing here but which should be mentioned because it exposes some of the processes of translation. One of Nabokov's characters speaks of the original poem as a tree casting a unique shadow. The translator is someone who constructs a ramshackle device looking nothing like that tree, but which somehow contrives to cast the same shadow. While translating these poems I devised a heterogeneous scaffolding of commentary generated by the shadow of the original on my own mind and culture. Krivulin welcomed this extra level of annotation and was keen that it should appear with the original. But, despite the best efforts of the publisher, traditional book type-setting proved inadequate to the extreme typographical challenges posed by that extrapolation. So it is left to readers to generate its equivalent in their own imagination.

Michael Molnar

I   Art. Fragonard[1] (Fr.) The Toilet of Venus

Photoreproduction in the women's dormitory of the Svetlana[2] works

has the radiance of a solar hand
not penetrated here – not touched the photo
reprint ripped from a glossy magazine[3]
art reproduction's mystery is – the pity

for that hand which smoothed the corners out
which pressed the miserable thumbtack in
the dormitory walls – and walls turn bright
become as if attractive – become almost human

like a soapbubble the painting swells –
fragonard's creampink bath-house orgasm
fills this desolate siberia of a dwelling
with clouds of aphrodisiac steam

here they spend the night, have breakfast – but
they don't live here . . . waiting, that's all:
tomorrow, perhaps tomorrow will change the lot
air   heart   and world beyond the wall

past life is crumpled up in a ridiculous lump
or is salvation's mystery – of the flesh?
therefore the typographical hint's not crude
to indicate the bliss of the Good Sunday bed

1   FRAGONARD: Born 1732 in Grasse, centre of French perfume manufacture.
2   SVETLANA: Light bulb factory in Leningrad. Predominantly girls and
    unmarried women work on its assembly lines at tasks which require especial
    manual dexterity. The name refers to 'light' (svet) and also to the heroine of
    Zhukovskii's romantic ballad who pines away waiting for her betrothed.
3   OGONËK: 'Fire' (diminutive-hypocoristic). A weekly illustrated magazine.

11   The Chinese Palace at Oranienbaum [1]

Colour artphoto (dim. 1.5 x 2 m.). Photographer B. Smelov.
Accounts dept. of the A.V. Lunacharskii factory[2]
of folk musical instruments.

crossing the keyboards of the palace
past a stock of tipsy harpsichords
where an inflammable and tangerine
cloud of pollen hangs suspended
burning on a mirrored draught
in a frozen formal blaze
you can't understand how come
you landed here? and by what right
antiques flourish in this place
but as for time – time's drying up
it's in grey tufts made out of minutes
that are used to stuff up cracks
it's in the eyes the colour of straw
now flaring up aflush with lust
now changing to a swarm of blackamoors
now like a porcelain chinaman
rhythmically nodding his head
in dissatisfaction: you, my friend,
look like a foreigner, not at home –
and so illtimed, so out of place! well
alright then, just shade your eyes

1   THE CHINESE PALACE AT ORANIENBAUM: A masterpiece of rococo archi-
    tecture built by Rinaldi in 1768 for Catherine the Great. Oranienbaum,
    now Lomonosov, is famous for its porcelain.
2   A.V. LUNACHARSKII FACTORY: Produces imitation folk musical instru-
    ments for which there is no demand – balalaikas, low quality guitars etc.
    Lunacharskii was First Commissar for Culture during the early years of
    Soviet rule, and died in 1933 while ambassador in Spain.

III   Pushkin in the guise of Danko[1] illuminating people's path

brigade of monumental artists of the RSFSR art foundation[2]
decorative panneau in the central premises of the Gorkii kolkhoz
in the Poshekhonskii district[3]

o muse! but of the nine of you
which muse? I run the risk
of getting lost and going astray
in such backwoods   in such murk
where nothing but a single guide
kindling the light of one-eyed reason
is leading a blind multitude
along the track of mythical narration:
anecdote on anecdote
a few mere shrubs – and lo, a vase
go back or forwards, what's the odds
here it's everything at once

yesterday where Tomorrow slept
posthumous and graveyard 'plus'
smoke of the Tsarskoe Selo landscape[4]
nursing home of the national muses
some sort of military cudgel fame
features of a departed poem –
can you inspire into its cooling limbs
the spirit of the Economic Achievements Show?[5]
once resurrected it'll groan out
that the future – is behind us
courage! in his prophetic clutch
he'll seize the heart out of his breast

and lit by its magnesium glow –
each like a damp newspaper page –
quiver illumined by the poet
shaggy tattered shreds of faces
we are laid down as rows of words

and file before him in the form of quotes –
nocturnal inspiration we transmute
into the respiration of a crowd
like marchers on a mass parade
we do the rounds of sacred spots
where he a fabled schoolboy sang –
and silent was the nightingale

1 DANKO: hero of Gorkii's romantic story, The old woman Izergil (1896).
   Danko tears out his heart which then burns like a torch illuminating the
   path of a tribe lost in a dark hostile forest. In the aesthetics of socialist-real-
   ism Danko is a symbol of the revolutionary leader sacrificing his own life for
   the happiness of the masses.
2 BRIGADE OF MONUMENTAL ARTISTS: As a rule large orders are allotted by
   the Art Foundation and executed by brigades of unknown artists working
   together on the assembly line principle.
3 POSHEKHONSKII: Signifies 'a backwoods', extreme provinicalism'.
4 TSARSKOE SELO: now Pushkin, home of the Lyceum where he studied.
   Before 1917 the poetical capital of Russia, linked with Akhmatova,
   Annenskii, Blok, Gumilёv, Mandelshtam. Many monuments to military
   victories erected there in the late 18th c.
5 ECONOMIC ACHIEVEMENTS SHOW: VDNKh, Exhibition of the Achieve-
   ments of the National Economy (formerly Agricultural Exhibition). The
   architecture of its pavilions and installations is a model of tastelessness on
   a colossal scale – a monument to the imperial pretensions of the Stalin era.

IV Principal Inter-District Specialized Tumour Hospital No. 2 (Manilov's former estate)[1]

*Xylogravure by art. Rakov from the series
'Rightflank health services'*[2]

*office of ass. chairman of the medical staff
trade union's regional committee*

a hilltop house
ionic portico   four white
pillars

soiled light and flashes in darkness
like a fairground booth
pneumatic birdflight of pellets

a throb and whirr
a car drives up to the entrance
a doctor leaps out

between leonine plastercasts heavenly thunder roars
then a silence
spurt of footsteps – turn away or hide your head

in a mass of gauze
of communal mourning for comrades
there drowning

amid the sea of day with its shimmering floor
on the hilly beds
where the pagan temple of life is swaying

only draw breath
a bit more freely   deeply   broadly –
façade will collapse

breast will subside into the heart's depth
nothing but four
radiant pillars remain intact

1 MANILOV: One of the characters in N. V. Gogol's 'poem' *Dead Souls*. A symbol of an extremely sentimental, complacent, hair-brained, head-in-the-clouds attitude towards life. Manilov's manor house is an image of ultimate incongruity and desolation. Its appearance in no way corresponds to the cultural pretensions of its owner.

2 RIGHTFLANK HEALTH SERVICES: In Soviet medicine, as in other spheres of life, the notion of 'socialist competition' exists. Those medical establishments whose basic indices (e.g. mortality figures etc.) are best, are considered to be leading or 'rightflank' (official terminology adapted from military usage, insofar as in the formation of army units the tallest soldiers stand on the right).

v   View of the Leningrad Montmartre

Work of an unknown artist, taken down at the demand of the
examining committee of the Governing Body for the Arts, in the
process of censoring an exhibition of non-conformist artists.

The title is a supposition, the work itself being lost without trace,
all that is known is its verbal description, extremely contradictory,
however, and none too trustworthy, insofar as the public were by
and large creative people and more concerned with their own
problems, which is forgivable when one takes into account their
present ambiguous situation.

it's over now. savage jackfrost
has loosened hold. you almost fly
the cupolas tin parachutes
the rooftops spanned as wings –
and suspended like Laputa
paris radiates constant light

as if they hadn't ever shut
printing presses or frontiers –
fleamarket books piled on the street
the dealer in his fluttering cape
over a maelstrom of names
immobile, bow your head:

in flitterglints and interglimmers
of the lexaemic matter –
a seething mêlée and the summer,
redhot shimmering abundance
of women in rustling dresses
immersed in lace

festival of lines and colours
odours   desires   stars
growing more and more ecstatic
in the pictures executed lifesize –

air more blue with carbon fumes
rat's tail growing more pale

under ground – at the centre
of the World – it'll sign the canvas

(1984 – the Year of the Rat)

NOTES FOR GALLERY VI

1 A. SHILOV: One of the most odious of Soviet artists, a portraitist who exploits the devices of hyperrealism in his struggle against so-called 'cosmopolitan and modernist' tendencies in Soviet painting. Exponent of extreme nationalist ideas.

2 IL'YA GLAZUNOV: Older rival of Shilov. Also an exponent of the 'nationalist idea', though, to be fair, in a more aesthetic form stemming from Russian art of the turn of the century. Extremely popular in wide circles unconnected with art.

3 MANEZHNAYA SQUARE: One of the central squares of Moscow, near the Kremlin. In the Manezh building on this square is the Central Exhibition hall of the Artists Union. At the end of 1979 a personal exhibition of Glazunov's work was held here – the queue extended for several kilometres, encircling the building.

4 ALL-RUSSIAN etc.: Voluntary organization once linked to the 'nationalist idea'.

VI Art. Shilov.[1] Portrait of Il'ya Glazunov[2] against the background of Manezhnaya Square[3] during the exhibition of his work

corridor in the premises of the Pskov section of the All-Russian Society for the Protection of Monuments of History and Culture[4]

and our history too deserves
a brighthaired brush
and blue-eyed paints
what is it otherwise? a graceless bellow
waterless the volga   woodland leafless
soul – pawned off and in deposit accounts

artists are a merry tribe
but by their very nature strangers,
they don't share out the spiritual bread –
and folk have been starved on the naked
forgetful earth where they once lived
we are different under our own sky

but the Craftsman will be found
the painted eyes of an ikon
will open – and will gaze into the soul
will widen – and will elevate the spirit
not forms – but formal icons
will drift out of the matinal russian mist

twisted in a muddled queue
round the square, in twos and threes
you can sense the buckling tight
of army belts

let shame of human dearth be all around –
there is a soil that's stocked with heroes
in the viviparous veins there is a sky
tucked beneath the shirt!

VII   Art. Savrasov.[1] The Rooks Have Flown In

*copy done by students of the Intermediate Art School at
the I.E. Repin institute as sketching practice*

*kitchen of a communal flat[2] in a house in Peski[3] previously
rented out by A.G. Snitkina-Dostoevskaya[4]*

on feltsurfaced fields
curtailed at the top and in the distance
the wind revels

prickly sparse nap
of last year's lightblue grass
in places on the low hills

from early youth
get used to it – till death you'll have to
look at this scene

demanding nothing from an earth
bare and frostbitten
only sympathizing secretly

a hopeless drunk, the teacher
takes them out sketching
to the state farm 'Shushary'[5]

the rooks have flown in, naturally!
have settled, ruffling feathers
each – not at home to itself

each one tormenting space
in its own way – tearing out
a clump of its own truth

1   SAVRASOV – Famous Russian artist of the second half of the nineteenth century. His masterpiece, 'The rooks have flown in', is one of the most popular paintings in Russia. He died of alcoholism.

2   COMMUNAL FLAT – After the revolution the majority of flats in Petersburg became 'communal', that is, several families were moved into them. The construction and allotting of separate flats only began in Khrushchev's time. Communal flats survive today in the centre of the city. Characteristic of them is a certain type of day to day existence and of human relationships.

3   PESKI – District in the city centre, not far from the Smol'nyi. Low-ranking civil servants and retired officers lived there. Famous for the number of rented properties.

4   SNITKINA-DOSTOEVSKAYA – The writer's second wife. After F.M. Dostoevsky's death she invested the money received from the sales of her husband's books in the purchase of dachas and rented accomodation.

5   SHUSHARY: State farm near Leningrad, on the road to the town of Pushkin. In autumn students work here in the fields, in the spring they come here to sketch. The name of the rat Shushary, well-known in Russia, is from a children's story by Aleksei Tolstoi.

VIII   Art. Deineka & Samokhvalov.[1] Boris
Pasternak reads poems from his new book
Second Birth[2] to workers of the Sverdlov engine
sheds, undergoing in the course of the reading
a series of wondrous but rule-determined
reincarnations – first into a 'JS' locomotive,[3]
then into a thoroughbred akhaltekinski[4] racehorse.

Museum of Railway History. Hall of the 1st 5-year plans.[5]

long decades – yet so many words
unspoken   overgrown with fungus
highcheeked the Hero and lowbrowed
but iron nodules pass across
his face – a locomotive streaks
elbows continuously on the move,
untamed nature runs astray
in a motif from pasternak

the stammering urals rear their heads
whistle of splintered cobblestone
on either side, at waysplit of
a track to oil or to gold
the miner's soul is spotless, washed
in rivulets of School for All[6] –
but poverty grows at the rate
and in proportion to the haul
of subterrranean goods to light . . .

and the word, a rare bird, yearns
having said 'yes' to blurt out: 'no!'
no, I'm not measured by a Five Year Plan![7]
its dimensions are more vast
than is my incomplete construction:
up chalkhills with a freight of coal
a goods train crawls. below, confusion

down in the quarry – hardly will
the poet on a rostrum manage
to lift his voice across such youthful,
smokedimmed, hostile expanses

so let him run away and hide
unnoticed with his happiness,
gulping down steamengine smoke
in a hotel during the asiack evening
let him weep and tremble at a letter
from a woman who imagines that
in his bearing he should be compared
to a fiery steed, bogged down in mud

1 DEINEKA: Artist, became famous in the 1930s. His art is of a constructivist
   nature and is distinguished by a certain 'machinism' in the depiction of
   people. Considered one of the leading exponents of construction-site
   inspiration by which Stalinist art of the '30s was popularized.
   SAMOKHVALOV: Portraitist, contemporary of Deineka. Obliged during the
   '30s to participate in the execution of collective paintings reflecting new
   social demands and tendencies in art.

2 SECOND BIRTH: Collection of Pasternak's verse of 1930–31, reflecting the
   theme of renewal and rebirth of the poet's soul under the influence of
   increased social activity stimulated by the inspiration of the first Five-Year
   Plans.

3 'JS': Heavy locomotive named in honour of Joseph Stalin.

4 AKHALTEKINSKI: The most pureblooded central Asian breed of racehorse,
   distinguished by its speed and endurance. In her poem, 'The Poet',
   Akhmatova wrote of Pasternak: 'He has compared himself to the eye of a
   horse.'

5 IST 5-YEAR PLANS: Plans of industrialization and cultural revolution
   intended to change the whole psycho-social structure of Soviet people.
   First 5-year plan 1929–32, the second 1933–37, were completed ahead of
   schedule.

6 SCHOOL FOR ALL: *Vseobuch*, Stalin's campaign to wipe out illiteracy.

7 'Can't I be measured by a five-year plan . . . ': Line from Pasternak's poem
   'To a Friend' (1931), an exhortation to lose oneself in the general current
   of a people vowed to happiness and the 'earthly paradise'.

IX Photograph of an unknown adolescent,
printed on thick, coarse-grained paper with a
high silver content and framed in a crude,
home-made wooden frame; the tone of the work
deep brown, the frame whitewashed.

anonymous imitation painting on plywood, intended as an
advertisement for a private photo studio now closed down

hangs in the Planning Dept. of Acommodation Resources Committee
No. 11
Acc. Fig. No. 18000508053

will we find poverty, not having sought it?
it vanishes – but will return again
there was a time made only of the present
unstable situation with no past
everything that was – was here, not somewhere.
there was time: they stole it, looking round
from newspaper they lived to newspaper
curious that they remained alive.
endless timber woodsheds
smelt of birchbark freshly stripped –
that surely is the secret smell of heaven
the pungent smell of splintered wood!
scream of a saw carried across backyards
soft sawdust caucasus grew beneath the trestles
a sense of hunger bordered on delight
on the otherworldly, the outlandish,
on such altitudes beyond the clouds
that one could simply stand forever – head
thrown back – like in the happy photograph
faded from its time behind shop windows

x   Art. Vatenin.[1] Portrait of the Leningrad
poet Aleksandr Kushner,[2] behind whose back is
clearly visible an engraving executed in the '40s
of the last century, representing a panoramic
view of the Nevskii Prospekt from the Main
Staff Headquarters to the Fontanka.

*Herzen St.[3] Leningrad section of the Artists Union, room of the
purchasing commission of the All-Russian Art Lottery*

when the poet bespecked with eyes
but all bespectacled, in the lenses' rollcall
catches a distorted silence
and the nexus where light-weaves intersected

when sliding down a fiery sinusoid
he strives to gain a foothold and to freeze
petrified before the biblical cloud
in which the Voice's being begins

then what's the point of verse? its reader's dead
and only posthumous reading trickles on
as if the parabolic mirror were turning[4]
on the Duma building's tower

what's the difference where they beamed it to
the illustrious order from the Winter Palace –
if only Tsarskoe! – but light behind the words
and dark and light did not have any end

everything passed into the future – seemed eternal
and the Lord revealed the Book unto the flock
fused it literally with human breath
to the extent – that Word too was made flesh

gospel according to John, the first two verses –
possibly the single nucleus
of all our powers of speech, of all our cursed
literature disseminating goodness

at war against the Russia of nicholas,[5]
however heartfelt Herzen,[6] however right –
a language reigned there over natural forces
and the word was a bond – and there was a heliograph

now one reads kushner through a magnifying glass:
the russian-speaking world has such short sight
who can make out – a metaphor? an act?
tiredness? courage? fright?

1   Contemporary Leningrad artist of the postwar generation. One of the first
    to use elements of a 'retro' style in his art.
2   Contemporary Leningrad poet. Known for the cultural-satirical tendencies
    of his art. In his poetry allusions to 19th-c. literature are frequent. Uses old
    engravings, often with views of Petersburg, as objects of description. This
    poem uses a famous engraving from the middle of the last century.
3   One of Leningrad's central streets, at right angles to Nevskii Prospekt.
    Formerly Bol'shaya Morskaya. The Artists Union is situated here, in its
    hall Vatenin's work has been exhibited.
4   In the middle of the last century an enormous mirror was installed on the
    building of the Petersburg magistracy, or Duma (from the word 'thought'),
    for the transmission of light signals from the Winter Palace, where an anal-
    ogous mirror of lesser dimensions was installed, to the tsar's summer resi-
    dence, Tsarskoe Selo, 20 kms. away. This was a unique light telegraph
    which functioned until the end of the last century.
5   The reign of Nicholas I (1826–55) was known as an age of reaction and of
    the government's struggle against the social influence of the press and of
    artistic literature. A time of centralization and of the bureaucratization of
    all social relationships.
6   One of the fundamental ideological opponents of the nicholine system.
    Illegitimate son of the aristocrat Yakovlev, the surname Herzen being from
    the German 'heart'. In 1848 he emigrated from Russia and laid the founda-
    tions of the émigré Russian revolutionary press.

XI Art. Fedotov.[1] Pasteboard with a sketch
for an unrealized genre canvas:
  'Morning of a Petersburg lady
      or
  Annunciation 1848'

*Copy executed by an unknown artist during the '20s of this century,
the original lost in the course of the evacuation*

Collection of the Perm State Gallery

glory to caesar! and glory to God in the highest!
kettledrum morning. a bell calls to matins. a mouse in the corner
the stove has gone cold. the stoker arrived. digs out the cinders
by each entrance gate a janitor rises
resting on a broom and standing slumbers

power strong and stable, posed like Pallas
resting on a spear, her chest bearing a numbered badge[2]
but in polar Athens during its lenten springtime
bones are racked. the Crucified stares from his ikon-case
splinters of birchback in the furnace burst into flame

'Maiden-Mother of God' starts up then falters, a voice calls
the chambermaid (oh bother, my tongue's in a knot, it won't utter
God's word): Palashka! a torrent of bare heels scuttles
drowning the servants' quarters, the hall . . . – (how downcast
    I feel
in the mornings, if only you knew – until the mysterious murmur

in the heart falls silent, a night chill's final trace)
humankind is composed of forebodings and mortal abysses –
that was either written by gogol or said by a certain elder
returned from our Saviour's tomb to repose in peace
crowning his columbine years with a halo of gold
dress me, palashka! church must already have started
the Annunciation service, icefloes shuffle outside the shutters

I dreamed, a triangular dream: an arcade, the garden of my
    parents
but deep down as if in a pit and yearning for daylight –
how could it be reached? how could it be placed back on earth?

I am powerless, dressed in white, I am kneeling
leaning over the pit, I can hear: from the abyss
'Maria! Maria!' they call – and the trees are no longer in sight
either wet clay below me or else it's like shoemaker's glue
something sticky, that breathes ... I am seized with terror, my
    hands

immersed as in dough – and the dough is swelling up
in anguish of spirit I woke: where am I lying? on the street
cobblestones! naked and in the cold and the disgrace –
a janitor is leaning over me waving his iron broom
'Rubbish, lady ...' – he weeps – and there are tears in his beard

'rubbish ... rubbish' – he mutters, and sweeps me like paper
    aside
rustling I wake – am I really crushed up in a lump?
and why should I dream this? the cold streaming up from my feet
for some reason bursts in my heart like the horde of mamai[3]
in a sea of feltboots, kneeboots, jackboots

how close it is – there inside me – a fug of warm breath!
Pelagaia, I look at you, and it's dark all around:
translated you are 'of the sea' – what's a name? just a sound
but I look at you – in awful oceanic expanses
immersed, I sink down to the seabed, I drown

1   FEDOTOV: Famous Russian artist of the time of Nicholas I. Ex-officer. Worked in the genre of scenes from everyday life. Painter of socially critical pictures. Died not having completed many projects, having gone mad. In 1848 he was already mentally ill. He is considered a victim of the stifling cultural climate of Nicholas I's time.

2   A NUMBERED BADGE: Caretakers or janitors in old Petersburg were mainly Kasimov Tatars. They wore white aprons with a big badge on the breast on which was indicated the number of the house they served. Often they combined their duties with the functions of secret police informers.

3   MAMAI: Tatar khan whose enormous army was defeated on the field of Kulikovo in 1380 by the forces of Dmitrii Donskoi.

XII Art. K. Bryullov (Bryullo).[1] Hercules
tearing off the poisoned costume on crossing
the Russo-Prussian frontier in 1849. Posthumous
self-portrait on the premises
of the Crown Customs.[2]

*Reception room of the Director of the Kaliningrad Visa
and Registration Office*

leaden   glowering quadristratified
hung the cloud – back there thunder pounds,
germany already? – and life's refurbished
ah, at long last! – and he springs down to the ground

from petersburg they had travelled in silence.
sown with beetroot the livonian fields
slowly stretched away. a lilac glimmer
grew in the west. resiliant material

tightened on the bosom of the fellow traveller:
'are you artists truly unacquainted with the tender passions?'
silence. – 'at wayside inns oppressed by officers
neither rooms nor horses can be obtained!'

silence. she took offence and went into a sulk
plucked at her passport, in her annoyance cut short
the customs officer – but suddenly the highway
breath and every movement narrowed

can it be Germany? his face seemed lifeless
she saw – and gasped out at the sight
around the artist in a demonic double ellipse
as a bloodsoaked interrogation mark

his mantle twisted round him like some beast.
his hat flew off and beltstraps scintillated –
and skin, an old man's, cold and indigo,
like the sea which shimmered in the distance

drenching her with unearthly cold
he is naked   he cried out about a poisoned town
where what was best lay buried beneath false gold
as cooling cinders . . . better not go to ruins

to pay respects to the Coliseum's remains,[3]
better if the Academy hadn't sent him –
then at least they'd not have given him reason
to set his hopes on Beauty which could not save him

better not to see the hands of maidens
stretching out towards the clustered grapes
o crimson light! should there be nervous laughter?
or sobbing, on the journey up

returning? – but from there, from the official
stitchwork constricting soul inself beneath a uniform[4]
I will not take the slightest scrap of green
nor a locket of the healer Pantaleimon![5]

like stridulant articulated insects
around him interjections circulated . . .
'his life's impossible', – she thought – and sunset's
afterglow widening in the West replied

1 KARL BRYULLOV (Bryullo) was Italian by origin, but born in Russia. The most popular commercial painter in Russia during the 1840s. Painter of official portraits, scenes from society life, canvases on biblical themes. Court artist, graduate of the Academy of Art, brilliant master of academic techniques. He was small, a freak with an enormous, handsome head and short legs. He loved dressing up and draperies. At the end of the 1820s he lived in Italy on a grant from the Academy of Art. Returned to Russia and despite his pleas was not allowed to leave until 1849, on the pretext of going to Madeira for medical treatment. In the same year he died in Italy. Legend has it that on crossing the Russian frontier he stripped naked in order not to take anything Russian with him.

2 The allegorical title corresponds to Bryullov's style.

3 This refers to Bryullov's first journey abroad in the 1820s.

4 Court artists were obliged to work in full-dress uniform if they crossed the threshold of the Hermitage. The green stitching on full-dress uniform indicated that one belonged to the palace department. Artists were regarded as civil servants of this department.

5 In the orthodox church Pantaleimon is the patron saint of medicine. The sick wore his image in the hope of help.

Katia Kapovich
(21 June 1960–)

Translated by Richard McKane

KATIA KAPOVICH was born in Kishinev, Moldova. She emigrated from the Soviet Union, where she had been a member of a literary dissident movement, in 1990. She lives and works in Cambridge, Mass. with her husband, the poet Philip Nikolayev and their child Sophia. In 1993 and 1994 she taught Russian literature at Boston College. She and her husband co-edit a new English-language poetry magazine, *Fulcrum*.

Her poems are tiny narratives, exquisitely crafted, rhymed and quite complex. Her first book, *Den' angela i noch'* (Day and Night of the Angel), was published in Israel in 1992, and the poems in this collection written in the 1990s come from that book. She also writes fluently in English which proves that Katia Kapovich is that rarest of poets: one who is bilingual. I'd like to present here one of her English poems, which was published in *The Antigonish Review*:

A Death

My first love died in the Afghan war,
but not from bullets, not by the hands of Mars.
He drowned while swimming in Ferry Lake.
That's why they didn't bring him back to us,
but buried him there, in the sands of the desert.
The soldiers did not shoot into the air
eighteen times, which was his quicksand age.
No drums broke the sirocco silence.
My first love died because he couldn't swim.
They had marched him across the desert for two weeks,
he saw a lake, a blister on the lips
of the earth. He sneaked out to the bank
and jumped into the water. Then his heart stopped.

A water-nymph looking a bit like me
pulled him by hand ashore. There he lay
on dry mignonette and watched the clouds
marching across the desert sky.

Her interest in narrative poetry (she wrote a 'non-Soviet' long poem at the age of eight) led to a book-length poem, *Suflior* (The Prompter, 1998) and to the statement that if Mandelstam had survived he would have written a brilliant narrative poem. It is Mandelstam in particular who shines through her poetry and in another English poem 'Blacklisted Titles' she describes a clandestine visit to the banned books section of the USSR Academy of Science Local Branch:

Those were the days when *Lolita*,
Mandelstam's *Voronezh Notebooks*,
let alone a Solzhenitsyn, could earn you
a couple of years in jail . . .

It is always exciting to find a new living poet, totally original, but with echoes of past voices and with a strong resonance of survival. Katia once e-mailed me that if she doesn't write for a long time she feels ill. Her second book, *Proshchanie s shestikrylymi* (Farewell to the Six-Winged, 2001 – a reference to the six-winged seraph in Pushkin's poem 'The Prophet'), which is an equally rich collection, has been followed by *Perekur* (Smoke-Break, 2002). Since she now travels to Russia regularly and is published in the best Russian magazines, she will not completely live off 'the bitter bread of exile' as Boris Poplavsky did, as Joseph Brodsky did. She writes in the concluding poem of this collection:

We did not fall – we did not go mad.
Restraining ourselves from words of comfort,
nonetheless let's give thanks for the time
of the year, for these damp steps
which have counted our footsteps over and over.

Richard McKane

Farewell

The soul has still not returned from the garden beyond the
    grave
and the glass lets through the flood of the pale heavens,
only black lime trees have gathered behind a black fence –
they have come to look at your madness.

There was a smell of spring and sweet petrol
from these smashed roads battened down with cord
to which God flew down as a blue pen to say farewell
to the son and take away the earth from underfoot.

But everything from treachery to the figure of physical death
was beaten out there on the frozen tablets of the river
where some boy, touching the earth with his knees,
screamed at your back: run from here, run.

Journey

Tell me, mocker, my double,
can it not be that it was so sad?
Take this unrhetorical question
and come out of the mirror confusion.
Lift your eyebrow in surprise
as one lifts a wine glass by the bottom.
This is how people look at yesterday's love
and the heart beats a little quicker than necessary.
Oh come down to a shadow still unclear
from your little belfry:
we'll sit by the doors' threshold
and squeeze together and bend our knees inside.
You will not forbid a beautiful death!

Then let's saddle the webbed goose
and sail over the misty roofs
on our round of carefreeness and sadness.
The yellow windows are like honeycombs
and your city is a buzzing hive.
My star-gazer: look at the street lamps
in the angular lens of the streets.
So the world revolves round itself
as we sail through the fine autumn.
Then come down to these birds' acres –
the dry abbreviation of space.
Sing the wordless swansong
to the night-watchman in the yellow hut –
don't, don't let him suspect that it's awful
for me to die because I'm not used to it,
like a moth hitting the flame.

'This is the saddest of days in the year'

This is the saddest of days in the year
when no birds flock outside the windows,
when fish float up in the stagnant pond
and when the aspen is wet through.

When you and I flounder from morning
under the slanting rain dragging over the city,
and our conversation is like
a silent pact behind a stranger's back.

It is also the saddest
of Septembers, without a finishing touch.
The black umbrella of the acacia is so limp
that it can't hold the sky at the bus-stop.

The connection is broken as empty vessels pour into the void
as though the soul is coming out of the body,
but crossing yourself with a chill hand
you wash your hands – the choice is made.

Look in the face of fate from here!
Who will dare to argue that this is true –
that we are alive finally,
having put off death itself till tomorrow.

The connection of all times, all days, has collapsed,
but no one hears that and it means
that only you, my fledgling, are shouting about it
and only the black air sways inexorably at the window.

Traveller's Notes

What is the sky? The heather of spring stars
where the clouds advance like tanks,
flying home to the north
where the angels are like guests from a binge.
The houses are black as starling-boxes
and people resemble birds
and life and death are outwardly similar
like two colourless drops of mercury.
Their souls draw circles
below the heavens and feet trample the earth,
already shouldering their cross,
the end justifying the means.
Thus their faces look into the darkness,
freed from their flesh,
from faded portraits
and lonely gateways.
God help them in the doorways of the provinces
and let there be more light in the black day!

The birds fly off to the north,
eyes look after them just the same.
Eyes look past just the same,
as though measuring with their look
in the mirrored reflections of the shop window
another costume for their rumpled wings.
The trefoil of the traffic light blossoms,
once more beating the hot road surface
and the whole world in the angel's vision
is the size of a football.

'I do my accounts at night'

I do my accounts at night
with him whom I loved more than life.
I put out the golden lamp
so that it doesn't lure the moths,
so that light doesn't burst into the eyes
and the pupils don't squint.
I will show him heaven
and hell as Virgil never could
to Dante. Oh if only he would walk
after me, leaning on air,
to that shelter, that last resting place
where grass and sand are underfoot
and the river is like cigarette smoke.
And when we row through the mist
and make for home in the usual way,
then we realize that the boatman's drunk
and the ferryman has not had a ferry for ages.
Even the home is gone:

the walls have rotted to the brickwork,
only the star that shone after us
will be there in its usual place.
There's no need to return,
to return there, either separately or together.
Better for the bird to circle without a nest,
better from the back entrance in the doorway
to loom alongside an alien shadow
there on the mourning stair.
Then the floor will become a shattered feature.
Night will share our exile.

'Now the air is black as water'

Now the air is black as water
your party is starting.
Starting – be calm with your pain,
with this easy word 'never'.
You can celebrate your tin wedding anniversary
with your closed circle,
but you can never curse
your lonely homeland.
Meanwhile, the only world in the window
opens up to you in the evening
from the columns, frozen in a stupor between
the houses flying to meet you in the darkness.
The last, late guest
will come in first through the door,
throwing down his stick as he walks in
and already planting a mischievous kiss on my forehead.

'Something from an untidy Russian life'

Something from an untidy Russian life,
from homegrown truth in the trough,
from a dried bunch of grapes:
I dream of these since there aren't enough events.

I dream simply of circles in front of the eyes,
the harsh chords of alleys in perspective,
so that my face is suddenly flooded
with tears. This cloudburst stands in my throat.

The doors open in the morning of their own accord
like a book at the required page.
Then I dream of some little square without
a subject and then simply of water.

So the sense of loss is growing dull,
memory gradually rusts like a knife.
Even when I am dead I will dream sometime
of these eyes, greener than the river by day.

'Oh to live, to live not in the sad capital'

Oh to live, to live not in the sad capital,
to tend the dry vine,
together with it to cling to some windows
and kiss their wooden cross.
On the road's surface the skies
would reflect – an impossible blue,
and an unstuck sweet-wrapper
would float in a puddle at start of spring.
Everything would become simpler, more vile:

the screams of the jackdaws, the trolleybus bell
and the gallery of days racing into
the distance, where the smoke is like light columns.
And so we would go to bed early,
seeing the moon, chased by the wind
along the side of the naked road
like a halo torn off a passer-by.
And habit, like second nature,
would gradually take over
the soul, now lofty, then sullen,
then comforting life: the two of us.

Monologue for Two Voices

Midnight. Be quiet, doorbell,
you fool! I must hear in the night
the cold crawling off the freezing stove,
searching for me in the depths.
Someone is standing behind my back, I can't work out
who – but we both go up to the window,
both look: I – from here to the darkness,
he to the dark from outside.

Two. The two of us in the whole of January.
The late reveller will hide
in the entrance as in a hole
and not come out from there when there is a knock.
The ceiling is a vault nonetheless.
Life ricochets off these walls,
flying from the panes
and now it's not there, not around.

This is just a blind alley,
your scream simply cannot be heard through the walls,
it's just that he who has ears has grown out of the habit

of believing night voices,
there is a time for everything
and here all is comfort: death and shelter,
the tatters of pre-war sky
with a pale star somewhere.

How about the winter, the winter beyond the threshold,
hillocks without snow, puddles without ice –
you will not make a mountain out of a molehill
or sculpt your snowman.
The first said: 'There is no other life'.
'There is,' the other answered quietly.
The wind hooted like an owl in the chimney.
The night snuffed out the candle.

Here it is the place for all meetings. Not the station,
not the lonely jetty by the cliffs,
for there are no sea, no seagulls, no sleepers,
and there will be none
when you lift the bolt on the door,
moving in on someone who screamed under lock and key.
There were two of us in the night,
two plus-or-minus fate.

Sentence

This city knows everything about the first spring:
so gilded is the air, so tender the spring heat,
so sweetly I'll sleep to see somewhere
the beaten road and the poplars' guard.

Where to and why do these people in grey wander at dawn?
The wax, the sealing wax of the moon has sealed my hearing
and a little snow circles over a white officer,
white from this snow. And this is the first circle.

And the second is in ice like a winter lake
and now the blue Christmas trees burn around.
With a dry voice, not smeared with a tear
I say to myself: slam that door!

When the gun clicks you will not even hear
and you will fall on the snow while you have strength –
because you lit the candles, because of your cough and cold,
because of the cawing of crows, the blackness of ink . . .

Because it is not your shoulder caught in the door
and it's not for you to lie in the snowy grave.
Know that it's only for this – to be extracted
like an obsolete letter from your alphabet.

'Don't look for me where I haven't been'

Don't look for me where I haven't been for ages:
in old letters, in a cracked cup from a tea-set.
Tomorrow our friendship will be one hundred years old
but we will not go on about the nature of this funeral feast.

You and I will believe in everything this year:
in the devilry, in fortune-telling in coffee dregs,
in the blown dandelion, in that life will survive
without us, destruction will not be mortal.

You couldn't dream up any city in the world in winter
that is cleaner in disaster and more triumphant;
as a result all day I follow with your eyes
my shadow circling in the flat.

It gets out of the chair, approaching the window
where the clouds run like foaming horses.
Only thus, in no other way, can you look
in winter time from light to dark.

Let us commemorate this New Year's night with bread,
with a burnt-out candle in a cut-glass glass.
Let the soul leave an imprint on it
and let us sinners be forgiven. Amen.

'Parting makes simple sense'

Parting makes simple sense,
there's no special sense in it.
The air will be to blame,
the garden full of birds whistling.
The smoke and the strip of water
there by the mossy forest.
Even that the sunset cut
across the rows of pines.
It will turn everything into ashes
with the quiet oncoming of night,
so that in tormenting dreams
the eye should fall for
the thousandth time
to the keyhole of the world
not finding in the light
that which it sought in the dark,
aiming at the door with the little cross-key.

And you raise a pale blue
pupil in the summer sky.
You will not share life with me
and couldn't care less about freedom.
But there is a terrible truth
hidden in your madness.
As though you know everything
about everything. Even more than is necessary.

'We no longer read poems at night'

We no longer read poems at night,
don't drink bitter spirit from glasses.
The leaves that whispered to us in such alarm
have somehow become haughty.

The black wind no longer leads us astray
to hide in the garden under the half moon
and the night does not come to rescue us
from madness frozen on the windows.

Well, one could wish for no better settlement
for the dilapidated walls and for the shadow
on the floor. But we will accuse ourselves
only of treason, so as to have no one to forgive.

We will accuse ourselves of heartlessness
and that this blind anguish, which
we track even with closed eyes,
will beckon us more powerfully than bliss.

26 June 1990

'For this alien non-Russian summer'

For this alien non-Russian summer
I will give up half my anguish,
half my sleeplessness, delirium
and rough verbal husks.

This is what I say to myself while
the night throws a bone on the tablecloth
and does not believe in sober reasoning
nor in my dispassionate anger.

But once it catches on a word
and forces to be truly different
her with the high-strung eyebrows,
a little haughty in her meeting with disaster.

From the light slap in the face of the wind:
on the lips the shadow of a smile like a leaf,
on the lips, that are stiffer than an envelope,
their corners turned down.

'All the words are rubbed out and forgotten'

All the words are rubbed out and forgotten –
there's no one to repeat them any more.
I will not meet you again
on the smashed back stairs;

or there where the squares stand out
beyond the green velvet of the wings.
An angel looks down from above,
from the belfry with its plywood.

Let friends still write to the end
the chronicle of our temporary disasters, etc.,
in the houses extended as a train
where you and I do not exist.

But no one will ever know
how the dust swirls in the slanting ray
and the acrid, odourless smoke
burns the lips, the lips.

It's easy, Lord, for us to be like this,
to drink unsweetened lemonade.
To call the dry orange sunset
by Your name, having forgotten its name.

To die every new evening
in the crowd buzzing like a beehive;
there where the light heat of petrified streets
turns the waves back.

'Full of autumn yellow'

Full of autumn yellow
letters don't reach the addressee.
Smoke your white cigarettes
and imprint your footsteps on the stairs.
Take your soul away in the evil midnight
to the shower-baths and drink in grief.
Pity all those who from love
inclined to the side over the sea.
But do not die, do not die,
even if you fell out of windows.
It's just that the milk flowed over
and turned into a cocoon.

You just did not think it's hard
as a nut, this bare fortress
with street lamps in two ranks
along the boulevards and tramlines.

'September again, season of broken twigs'

September again, season of broken twigs
after the high, luxuriant summer.
But through this transparent retouching
you whisper 'forgive' to the eternal 'retro',
then you are surprised at the object's ability
to be cold-blooded, and somewhere you have begun
secretly to envy your own disasters,
that poverty where ends can't be met.

Something is directly missing for us,
like birds at the end of migration:
either the point of calculation is lost
or the aim is clean gone.
The sky is everywhere like water, but the heart
of the matter is not in space or the time of year
but in that we are people without kith and kin.
Address. Registered residence. Fate in our face.

It's clear that our home is not our castle
but a tower of Babel among the ploughed fields
with a sad view, inasmuch as it sees
everything: both the white horses on the wave's crest
and the Crusaders. The air is so wet
that you can't breathe in or out.
Well, swallow this unsalted porridge
not with a spoon of salt but a troubled tear.

Let's say that we are grateful for the derision
with which, my country, you equate us with the rabble.
We did not fall, did not become the target
in some game – we did not go mad.
Restraining ourselves from words of comfort,
nonetheless let's give thanks for the time
of the year, for these damp steps
which have counted our footsteps over and over.

Notes on Contributors

VLADIMIR BASKAYEV was born in northern Caucasus in Russia, where he graduated from the University of Foreign Languages. There he worked on translations of Akhmatova and Daniel Andreyev. He left the Soviet Union for the UK in 1988 and has recently graduated from London Institute: Camberwell College of Arts. He lives in London and works as an artist.

MICHAEL BASKER is Head of the Russian Studies department at Bristol University. He has written extensively on the Acmeist poets Akhmatova and Gumilyov, contributing the introduction and notes for *The Pillar of Fire*, Nikolay Gumilyov's selected poems translated by Richard McKane, and has been active in preparing the Voskresen'e edition of Gumilyov's works. Pushkin, the nineteenth century and Russian Symbolism are among his other research interests.

BELINDA COOKE was born in Reading in 1959 and took a degree in English and Russian at Liverpool University. Her PhD was on the influence of Mandelstam on Robert Lowell. She has researched Russian Symbolist poetry and has worked on translations of Vadim Andreyev, Vyacheslav Ivanov as well as Boris Poplavsky. She has been an English teacher since 1982.

KITTY HUNTER-BLAIR's many translations include Andrei Tarkovsky's *Sculpting in Time, Time within Time*, and the kino-roman *Andrei Rublev*. In collaboration with Jeremy Brooks she has translated plays by Ostrovsky, Chekhov, Gorky and Solzhenitsyn for the Royal Shakespeare Company, and works by Dostoevsky, Tolstoy and Chekhov for the BBC. In 1999 she did a verse translation and adaptation of Pushkin's *Tale of Tsar Saltan* for the Little Angel Puppet Theatre. For twenty years she taught Russian language and literature at Cambridge. For the better part of fifty years she has been on the committee of the Pushkin Club in London.

RICHARD McKANE is the translator of the *Selected Poems* of Anna Akhmatova (1989) and, with Elizabeth McKane, of Osip Mandelstam's *The Moscow Notebooks* (1991) and *The Voronezh Notebooks* (1996). More recently he has published a selection from Nikolay

Gumilyov's poems, *The Pillar of Fire* (1999) and, with Ruth Christie and Talât Halman, a selection of poems by Nâzım Hikmet, *Beyond the Walls* (2002). He works in London as a Turkish and Russian interpreter for the Medical Foundation for the Care of Victims of Torture.

MICHAEL MOLNAR studied the work of Andrei Belyi at the University of East Anglia and at Leningrad University, on a British Council scholarship during the mid-1980s. There he met Viktor Krivulin and worked with him on the translations of 'Poems on Maps' and 'Gallery'. He has also translated other contemporary Russian poets, including Arkadii Dragomoshchenko, Aleksei Parshchikov and Elena Shvarts (*Paradise*: selected poems, 1993, with additional translations by Catriona Kelly). He now works as Research Director at the Freud Museum, London.

About Survivors' Poetry

SURVIVORS' POETRY is a national literature charity, set up in November 1991 by four poets defining themselves as survivors of mental distress. Initially comprising a small group of writers and performers of poetry in London, it is now a national network of more than twenty writers' groups and 2,500 members across England, Scotland, Northern Ireland and Wales, with associates in the Channel Islands, France and the USA. Despite its expansion, the organization remains survivor-led. Of its present membership, paid staff, volunteers and advisors, more than 95% define themselves as survivors of mental distress. Currently, many of the member groups run autonomous programmes, producing magazines and pamphlets of their own work as well as running writing workshops or holding events. The organisation also has a registered office in London from which it runs a small literary imprint, produces the quarterly magazine *Poetry Express*, runs bespoke training courses and co-ordinates the national and London events programmes. Survivors' Poetry aims to work across the whole of the British Isles in partnership with local and national arts, mental health, community and disability organisations. Now in its second decade, the focus of the organisation's work remains very much on personal development and recovery, whilst its membership embraces people of all social and cultural backgrounds.

No one knows why at times of heightened emotion many people are compelled to write poetry, but often out of the pain of experience come poems that testify to the transcending power of the imagination; an expression of emotion that has universal resonance – a work of art.

For information please write to

Survivors' Poetry
Diorama Arts Centre
34 Osnaburgh Street
London NW1 3ND

SOME PUBLICATIONS FROM SURVIVORS' POETRY

Fresher than Green, Brighter than Orange
An anthology of poetry by Irish women living in London in 1999
Edited by Eamer O'Keeffe & Lisa Boardman

Under the Asylum Tree
An illustrated anthology of poetry
Edited by Jenny Ford, Colin Hambrook & Hilary Porter

From Dark to Light
An illustrated anthology of poetry
Edited by Frank Bangay, Joe Bidder & Hilary Porter

NIKOLAY GUMILYOV
The Pillar of Fire

SELECTED POEMS
TRANSLATED BY RICHARD McKANE
INTRODUCED BY MICHAEL BASKER

This is the first major selection to appear in Britain from one of the finest poets of the Silver Age of Russian literature. The rich, exotic poetry of Nikolay Gumilyov (1886–1921) draws on his extensive travels in Europe and Africa. Its deepest concerns are man's inner being and striving for spiritual fulfilment. He was shot in 1921, unjustly accused of complicity in an anti-Bolshevik plot. His poems were banned and were not published in Russia until the late 1980s. Richard McKane's fluent translations are complemented by a full introduction and detailed notes by the leading western Gumilyov scholar, Michael Basker. An appendix includes nine poems by Anna Akhmatova relating to Gumilyov.

'A God-inspired master-craftsman ... cut down
in the very morning of his poetic mastery.'

MARINA TSVETAYEVA

'What this publication represents, finally, is by far the best
available collection of Gumilyov's poetry in English,
both in terms of the quality, sensitivity and reliability of
the translations themselves, and of the comprehensiveness
of the accompanying notes. Both McKane and Basker
are to be congratulated on this impressive achievement'

JUSTIN DOHERTY

SLAVONICA